Simple  Biz360™

Timeless Business Tools

Jeffrey R. Mason

Published by BizBits, LLC, Saint Charles, Missouri, 63304
Printed in the United States of America.

For permission requests, write to publisher:
BizBits, LLC, PO Box 53, Cottleville, MO 63338

Interior Design by BizBits, LLC
Cover Design by Lorie DeWorken
Cover Photo by Michael D. Lode
Author Photo by Michael D. Lode
All other photos courtesy of BizBits, LLC records
Graphic designs by Bob Zelle

ISBN: 978-0-578-57032-7
Library of Congress Control Number: 2019913115

www.simplebiz360.com

Dedication

This book is dedicated to all the brave individuals who take the risk of starting and operating their own small businesses.

Overview

This book is designed to serve as a business resource guide.

In an effort to conserve your time and provide easy information retrieval, we utilize lists, bullet points, headers and brevity throughout. Our goal is to deliver a pleasurable reading experience within a layout design tailored for business use.

Improving your business results is the core of our efforts.

This is a business **Tool Book.**

Field Notes

"During my career, there have been few people that have impressed me with their ability to focus on the most important task to be successful: supporting their customers with honesty and integrity. Jeff was a colleague and a business partner for many years. Many of the business practices that I use today, I have learned from him. This book provides a roadmap to success. We all need tools to help us be the best business person we can be. *SimpleBiz360*™ will help you achieve your goals by providing concrete tools and direction for personal business growth. Use the tools and enjoy the results."

Gretchen Waterman, Vice President R&D Apparel & Gear
Wilson Sporting Goods Co.

"Jeff's book is an inspiration to all of us who are striving to make it in the turbulent waters of running a business. Rewards are many to those who can apply and direct the tools Jeff presents. Jeff embodies resiliency and integrity. His tools will help a business owner in his or her business and also in their personal lives."

Didier Villard, President and Owner
EuroGourmet and Technobake

"Mason has cracked the code to easily understanding, storing, accessing, and utilizing critical tools to help successfully run your small business. Wish I had this 20 years ago."

Rich Brown, Owner
Perpetual Marketing, Inc.

"An intuitive look into the steps needed to run a successful business. Jeff Mason reminds us of the things we should be focusing on daily. All we have to do is pull them out of our Tool Chest and give them a try!"

Nina Brundell, Owner
Kieck's Career Apparel

"I've had the pleasure of knowing Jeff for many years, and if I could sum up Jeff in one word it would be "Passion." Jeff is passionate about life, business, serving his customers, developing others, his family and his Faith. Jeff has done the work, lived the life of an entrepreneur, taken the risk and put his money where his mouth is so that you can bear the fruit of his experience. Are you ready to go to work? Open up one of the drawers in the Tool Box, grab a Tool and let's get started."

Kevin J. Moran, Vice President, People Development
WieseUSA

"I have been in business for over 20 years and I have had the opportunity to interact with countless salespeople, reps, sales managers, etc. Hands down Jeff Mason has been the most knowledgeable and impressive sales manager that I have ever met! This book is the Bible on how to run a successful business! This is *the* "Tool Box"...... Buy it!!"

James Horan, Sales Professional
Independent Sales Representative

"Jeff Mason is the consummate gentleman who prioritizes honesty, integrity and professionalism. I had the good fortune to work with Jeff when he was VP of Sales and have since seen him build a successful sales rep agency. His years on both sides of the business provide him the vision and insight to write this book. If someone starting or already pursuing a small business utilizes the tools Jeff has outlined, they'll avoid many of the pitfalls and assure themselves a successful business."

Greg Alexander, Owner
Manufacturer's Representative & Agency Owner

"Jeff Mason has been a client of mine for many years. As a fellow small business owner, I found his book brutally honest, filled with real life examples of small business successes and failures. Provided in a compact and easy to understand format, *SimpleBiz360*™ demonstrates how to run a client- or customer-focused small business.

Whether you are just starting a small business for the first time or you have been running your small business for 30 years, the tools, tips and guidance presented in this book should help you on your journey toward becoming a successful small business owner."

Kyle Reise, CFP®, CRPC® Virtual Financial Planner
LPL Financial

"Jeff is a passionate individual with a thirst for knowledge and self-improvement. He is a very successful small business owner who is constantly looking for ways to improve the results for his customers. He has created a comprehensive business tool chest for your reference. This book enables you to capitalize on his results and learn from some of his challenges. Taking care of your customer, providing outstanding communication and making sure you continue to focus on results are all hallmarks of Jeff's successful strategy. I am confident you will find this easy to follow and very stimulating as you develop your own path to success."

Michael Miller, President
GCE International, Inc.

"I am not a handy person. When I watch a carpenter, electrician or mechanic doing their work, I am always amazed at what they can accomplish. Much of their skill comes from having the right tools and knowing how and when to use them.

Jeff applies this idea to the business world. When I started my business, I had to learn a lot of things the hard way, through trial and error. Learning from others is so much better. Jeff gives us tools to use in our ventures. Like any other trade, we start as novices then improve with time. Having the tools and knowing how to use them will let business owners get a jump start (improve) on success."

Steve Crawford, Owner
Steve Crawford Trucking, Inc.

"Jeff Mason has been a "Rock Star" for our company. His vast business experience coupled with insightful industry knowledge has resulted in sound advice, and along the way, has ultimately helped our company grow to be more than ten times the size it was just ten years ago. Jeff lives the tools he teaches, he demonstrates the highest level of integrity, and his passion for small business is second to none."

Gregg Koenig & Scott Adams, Owners
Great Plains Uniforms

"We sat down and read the introduction to *SimpleBiz360*™, and we were hooked. Easy to read, right to the point, great format and even greater information for us busy entrepreneurs.

As a couple that decided 28 years ago to quit our corporate careers and head out on our own, we find the tips provided in *SimpleBiz360*™ both refreshing and important. Fresh insight from Jeff and *SimpleBiz360*™ is interesting and needed in this ever-changing business environment.

As we welcome our next generation coming on board, new challenges await us all. *SimpleBiz360*™ will be valuable for busy professionals to move their businesses forward into the future."

Dawn and Dave Giombetti, Owners
DMGroup, Inc.

"Jeff Mason is as experienced as it gets when it comes to all things sales and business. Entrepreneurs of all ages can benefit from the tried and true insights of **SB360** with results that happen as quickly as you implement what he says. In a world where college and traditional education are transforming, **SB360** is the education that will get you where you want to go."

Adam Mason, Owner
Mason Photography

Contents

Foreword

I had been working with an associate for several years. One day, he mentioned that a college friend of his was looking to make a change in his career and I should meet this individual. Well, people are always trying to do favors for friends, and I thought this was just another one of those things. I agreed to meet him as a favor to my associate.

So Jeff Mason came to my office to meet me. After a lengthy conversation, I knew we had to hire this dynamic individual. I did not care that he did not have any apparel manufacturing experience. I knew that he had a great foundation in business, was an excellent communicator, and would easily fit into our company. My instincts told me that he would be able to learn our business in a short time and make a great contribution.

I have not always been right about things, but I was right about Jeff. He was thrust into our company with no apparel experience and devoured information. He was like a sponge absorbing all he could about the apparel manufacturing processes. I could see he applied the techniques of his past experiences and teachings of various mentors and applied these to our business. It was not long before we were learning from him! We made a great team for many years, and I have not only come to respect Jeff as a business associate, but as a personal friend. Jeff has great business sense, and he is a fine human being with good character. He dramatically grew our business in a relatively short time span. He was respected and admired by individuals from our company, and especially customers. I was extremely sorry when Jeff moved on from our company to assume a major position with a new one.

We continued to stay in touch. Once he decided to leave the "corporate world" to start another small business venture, we talked many times about this new opportunity. I was flattered when he asked me to write a foreword for his new book which is focused on helping the small business owner succeed and prosper. To be honest, I was not surprised to learn about *SimpleBiz360*™ as Jeff's passion has always been advanced personal training and development. He loves to pass that knowledge on to other people. If you are a small business owner, this book will be your bible to improving your business skills and keeping your customers "delighted" so your business with grow and prosper.

Jeff's unique concept of a "Tool Book," or a "go-to" business guide to help operate a small business is a fresh concept and easy to work through, especially given today's hectic lifestyle. His business Tools are explained in a clear, concise, and easy-to-read method.

Even though Jeff has had over 30 years of varied business experience working for larger companies, and especially operating his own businesses, he learned early on in his career that "Third Party Influencers," or professionals whose experiences he could learn from, were vital in helping his success. Their experience, advice, failures, and training would enhance his career and shape his business life. I suggest that you let Jeff be your mentor and his book be a learning resource to help you build a successful small business. I believe you will be able to take away many suggestions to improve your business and avoid what Jeff calls those "Silent Business Killers" that have a negative impact on your business.

Good luck and hope you will glean some wonderful insights from this book to make you a better business person and in turn, your business a wonderful success.

Peter Scardino, Director of Sales
Oxford Apparel

The Nutshell

Greetings solopreneurs and small business owners.

My career has involved a fascination with observing, dissecting and understanding business conduct, with the intended result of becoming a more effective professional. The concept of getting better is truly the core element of this book. I learned early on that the key to achieving more was directly connected to improving business skills.

Products and services are sold, and the sales transaction is the end goal that companies desire. The information in this book will assist small business owners in achieving sales transaction successes by operating their businesses in ways that are appealing to customers. In a nutshell, these actions are the business **Tools** that *SimpleBiz360*™ focuses on. If companies do not operate in a way that pleases customers, all the marketing and sales efforts in the world will not deliver **Repeat** transactions or a steady stream of **Referrals**.

Although my career roots are in "Selling" and "How Selling Works," as time progressed, it became crystal clear that understanding "Buying" and "How Buying Works" are equally essential for business growth. *SimpleBiz360*™ is built on the premise that the vast majority of small business owners don't want to learn how to be professional sales representatives. *SimpleBiz360*™ will not focus on sales techniques or selling methods.

My primary focus is to help small business owners perform simple daily actions that compel intended buyers to make a purchase with your company. Satisfied customers will help your businesses grow through **Referrals** and/or **Repeat** business transactions. In the end, my sincere hope is that this book will help you do the following:

1) Discover more enjoyment in small business ownership.
2) Retain more of your hard-earned profits.
3) Get a better return on your investment of time and money.

Thank you for allowing me to share the following information with you.

Why & What

To understand why I present this book, please consider this information about small businesses.

A September, 2012 Small Business Administration (SBA) Office of Advocacy Report summarizes that according to the most recent United States Census (2010), there were 27.9 million small businesses in America. This figure equates to 99.7 percent of all US employer firms. The SBA defines a small business as any company with less than 500 employees. Drilling down further, small businesses with one person and zero additional employees are referred to as non-employers. The number of these one-person, non-employer companies was estimated to be just under 21 million.

My intention is not to bore you with numbers. Updated statistical information is hard to come by as the US Census is performed once every 10 years. Current data and reporting support one-person company ownership to be in that 20-21 million range. I am going to use a safe estimate that there are at least 20 million one-person companies operating in the US in 2019.

I share this information with you to emphasize that many, many people operate small businesses with an owner and zero employees. Current culture references call them "solopreneurs" or "one-person companies." Mine is one of these 20 million businesses. **I am with you and operate every day on the same playing field as many readers of this book.** For the past 12 years I have, and still do operate a sales agency that represents various manufacturers in an Upper Midwest territory.

Many of us financed our business using the equity from our home. Some of us borrowed money from banks, relatives or friends. Thousands of us turn to credit cards as we start from scratch and grow from a corner of our kitchen, basement, living room or garage. A few of us inherited the business as second-generation ownership. Millions of us are challenged every month to pay our household and business bills. We have much in common!

In my experience I find that very few one-person and small companies are connected to learning business tips from anyone other than family, friends or the School of Hard Knocks. Picking up a "third-party" business book or attending a skill-building seminar is not done very often by these 20 million solopreneurs. *SimpleBiz360*™ is my attempt to share some *simple* and *proven* business suggestions. Please consider the following:

- This is NOT a training book.
- This is NOT a sales book.
- This is NOT a motivational book.
- This is NOT a get-rich book.
- This is NOT a start-your-own-business book.
- **This IS a Tool Book.**

This simple **Tool Book** attempts to cover 360 degrees of basic situations common to running your small business. Think of these business ingredients (**Tools**) as being arranged in a **Tool Chest** with various drawers containing different **Tools**. Use the book like this: Go to a drawer…look for what you need…grab it…and try it. If you like it, use it. If not, then don't use it. Maybe another **Tool** can come in handy with another situation or customer.

How

This book is deliberately designed for quick, easy reading and fast information retrieval. This book will be augmented with weekly podcasts where each **Tool** will be discussed in more detail. Please visit **www.simplebiz360.com** for podcast details.

The modern day, one-person company has limited time to juggle life and work responsibilities. My hope is that the layout and content of this book can be used as a timeless, go-to guide for assisting in the operation of your business.

I embarked on writing this book 30 years ago. With the passing of each year, I realized that simplification is essential and appreciated when assisting another business professional. In the 21st Century, most of us do life in our mobile device society where information appears in 3″ x 5″ glass windows. Information is fast and fleets by only to be followed by another rapid stream of data, text and visual stimulus. When we switch from our mobile device to the big screens (TV), many of us are accustomed to seeing multiple information streams, or channels, appearing simultaneously in one fixed glance.

Gone is the public appetite and patience for long, intricate and complicated business methodologies. Our daily world moves fast, and a large portion of society elects to bypass and reject complex formulas and techniques to achieve a result. Although I grew up in and benefited from the "Methodology Era," times have changed and so must information delivery. My mission is to deliver these business **Tools** with brevity, clarity and effectiveness.

In my attempt to simplify the elements of small business, I have concluded that there are essential drawers to the business **Tool Chest**: **Core, Customer, Procedure, Service, Communication, Money** and **Improvement**. These are supported by and predicated on the foundation of communicating effective **Expectations**. After more than three decades of keen business observation and study, I am thoroughly convinced most every small business **Tool** can fit snuggly in these key drawers of the business **Tool Chest**:

Although *SimpleBiz360*™ is targeted to a primary audience of solopreneurs, I encourage medium and large businesses to review this information. Growing up in an era that invited small companies to "think BIG," I personally encourage big enterprises to "think SMALL." Sam Walton, founder of Wal-Mart, put it this way in *SAM WALTON Made in America*, "The bigger Wal-Mart gets, the more essential it is that we think small. Because that's exactly how we have become a huge corporation — by not acting like one" (1992).

Who

Why read what I have to say? Who am I?

I am a risk taker and a solopreneur like many of you. My financial start included combining a small credit union loan and a credit card. The total start-up debt for my company was $12,000. **I share this book from a common-thread perspective as we experience similar debt loads and perform many of the same duties on a daily basis.**

My roots are not glamorous nor prestigious. I was raised by good parents in a healthy family environment. However, I carved my own destructive path for a while and then found long-term direction through God, life experiences and advice. During my journey, I vividly remember sitting in my college Social Work class (know the exact seat and position against the wall) when my professor said the following:

"A wise man learns from his own mistakes.
However, the wiser man learns from the mistakes of others."

If only I heard that advice when I was 15 and not 20! I believe life experiences shape us through key, pivotal events and periods of time. Here is a transparent and brief summary of significant life moments that have formed my identity starting at the age of 16:

Identity Events

- Arrested numerous times as a juvenile.
- Graduated from high school (barely) in 1976.
- Pumped gas first year after high school.
- Lost driver's license for drunk driving.
- Hitchhiked and rode a bike for four years.
- Worked night shift in factory second year after high school.
- Cleaned a bar every morning after my night shift.
- Started attending college my third year after high school.
- Met my lovely wife in 1981 while hitchhiking. (Seriously.)
- Got married in 1983.
- Graduated from college with a Sociology degree.
- **Secured sales position (1984) in a Wall Street territory.**
- Became a Christian in 1987.
- Quit drinking in 1987. (Still sober…thank you God!)
- Welcomed two beautiful daughters in 1987 and 1989.
- Created a company with my father in 1990.
- Ran out of money two years later.
- Sold all my assets to pay bills.
- Borrowed $3,600 from my father-in-law for living expenses.
- Received food donations from church in mid-1992.
- Worked for ten companies from 1984–2007.
- Secured Senior Executive position from a consulting job.
- Tried starting companies two other times and failed.
- Lost $25,000 trying to start companies.
- Started my fourth company in 2008.
- Still operate this company in 2019.

Credibility

I realize that some business professionals might be inclined to discount the quality of this book. What I need the readers to understand is that my inspiration is **Improvement**. These bite-size suggestions are specifically written to 20 million one-person companies. *SimpleBiz360*™ is proven and tested. I don't claim to have all the answers, but I do have some.

My career path does contain several professional capacities that exposed me to quality training and best business practices. With that foundation, plus my dedicated focus to observing and studying workplace conduct, I am able to deliver applicable solopreneur skills from a parallel one-person company perspective. Sharing improvement-based operational skills has been my intentional career plan and journey.

The 10,000-Hour Effect

During my reading of *The Circle Maker* by Mark Batterson (2011), I was floored when I got to the chapter entitled "Persistence Quotient." Mark discusses Anders Ericsson's modern-day study of musicians conducted at Berlin's elite Academy of Music. The Ericsson study focused on the differences in average, good and elite performers on the violin. Paraphrasing the results, researchers found (innate abilities aside) that elite (World Class) violinists set the standard with a minimum of ten thousand hours of practice. Batterson highlights comments from Neurologist Daniel Levitin:

The emerging picture from such studies is that ten thousand hours of practice is required to achieve the level of mastery associated with being a world-class expert in anything. In study after study, of composers, basketball players, fiction writers, ice skaters, concert pianists, chess players, master criminals, and what have you, this number comes up again and again…No one has yet found a case in which true world-class expertise was accomplished in less time. It seems it takes the brain this long to assimilate all that it needs to know to achieve true mastery.

This information is not to imply I am world-class at any endeavor. However, I have conservatively invested 57,600 hours into deliberate learning, observation and recording of situational business events. The supporting math: 240 business days per year x 8 hours per day x 30 years = 57,600 hours.

My actual career reaches 75,000-80,000 hours (factoring in 10-12-hour days). Please rest assured this book contains time-tested, proven and **Timeless Tools** designed to benefit you.

One of my business heroes is Dale Carnegie. In 2017, I made a trip to his hometown of Maryville, Missouri. It was fantastic just to soak in the surroundings he called home. I continually marvel that a man with such humble beginnings could give the world so much useful information. His simplistic and powerful explanations impacted me from the moment I read them. I'll never be a Dale Carnegie, but I aspire to deliver my content with a small flare of his humility, enthusiasm and relevance.

Professional Capacities

1) Executive Vice President (one company)
2) National Sales Manager (two companies)
3) Director of Sales, Recruiting and Training (one company)
4) Salesperson (eight companies)
5) Business Co-owner (one company)
6) Sole Proprietor (one company/2008 – present)

There is a significant time during my career that is the clear catalyst for this book. Now, let's go back a few pages to the highlighted **(in black bold)** entry level sales position I began in 1984. This is where everything changed for me.

This career stop provided the spark for the **Tools** in this book.

Stop. Reboot.

The company that hired me for a Wall Street Sales territory was Lanier Business Products. Their business model mandated putting me through an extensive three-week in-house sales training program capped off by an intense week of additional training at headquarters in Atlanta, Georgia.

With all this training (four weeks) memorized (to the word), I was given a territory and paid $1,200 per month in the form of what they called a "draw." As the employee, I was responsible to pay the draw back before I could keep any commissions. For each sale, I received commissions. Any commissions I earned above that draw

14

payback, I kept as extra income. I would be terminated if I owed the company more than $4,200 in draw.

Here is what happened to me:

- Went through training September 1st – September 30th, 1984.
- Never used the training from day one, October 1, 1984.
- Thought I could "wing it" with my talking skills.
- Failure was constant and termination became imminent.
- An associate shared a success story in late 1984.
- The rep gave 100% of the credit to our training program.
- **Stop**: Inspired and curious, I **stopped** the way I was operating.
- **Reboot**: I started using my training the very next day.
- The training worked on call #1 and day #1.
- The training worked week after week and month after month.
- I became a frequent Salesperson of the Month.
- I became a frequent Salesperson of the Quarter.
- I became Rookie of the Year.
- My income rose dramatically.
- The verdict was in, loud and clear: **The training worked!**
- This training taught permanent and transferable skills.
- **Transferable business skills became everyday Tools.**

Everything changed when I followed the training and utilized my newly acquired skills. My regional manager realized I had gained an appreciation for the **Improvement** process. As a result, he encouraged me to adopt an appetite for additional third-party (non-company) training to further advance. Suggesting these **Third-Party Influencers** (**TPIs**) would enhance my career, he urged me to read a business book a month and enroll in Dale Carnegie courses.

TPIs changed my life even more.

TPIs

As my desire for additional training grew, I realized that the best business direction came from professionals who went down roads before me. These proven superstars offered sound and applicable advice. My role was to humbly read, listen, think and apply their suggestions.

In retrospect, I was foolish to think I could become successful on my own. When you read my brief life history since age 16, you quickly realize I was not exactly the poster child for doing things well. My first three to four months of business life only reinforced mediocrity.

From 1985 through 1989, my thirst for more training and professional development was as high as it has ever been to date. Courses, books, tapes...more books...more tapes. I took in all I could get. I basically ate and drank this stuff! I listened...I digested, I tried many suggestions. I grew and advanced because of these **TPI** heavyweights.

When I look at the totality of business advice I received from **TPIs,** there is one clear standout. Dale Carnegie impacted me more than any other resource. **Why?** I am convinced it was his simplistic nature and approach. He used understandable words. His observations were not complicated. His suggestions were easy on the mind and eyes, and they made sense. He was simple and effective. I committed to being like Dale. This book is written with that goal in mind: Give the reader easy, brief, simple concepts that can fit the modern grab-and-go society we live in.

By 1989, I was at my second company. I was in a national management capacity and developing a hearty hunger for more professional development. Involving myself with Dale Carnegie (DC) offices in New York City and Philadelphia, I was pursuing the call to be a DC trainer.

In addition, in 1988 I wrote and developed a pilot program for a computer repair company. I constructed a two-week in-house sales training program and created a 187-page sales training manual specific to this company. With this framework, I hired and trained 65 college graduates and doubled the company size in two years. In 1989, at the end of that two-year span, I made a decision to write a business book focusing on professional development.

- Only a small portion of this book is Jeff Mason.
- I followed **TPI** wisdom that shaped my business actions.
- This book redelivers **TPI** advice with small business relevance.
- *SimpleBiz360*™ is rooted in situational observation.
- **Timeless Tools** can benefit current and future generations.

Lastly, I was humble enough to let **TPI** professionals into my career story. My hope is that you will allow me to become a source of **TPI** in your business story. I encourage you to roll out the welcome mat and let some of these **Tools** help you in your daily operations.

Takeaways

In 1985 my regional manager gave me one of the best pieces of advice I ever received. In the spirit of "Pay It Forward," here it is, paraphrased:

With every business book you read, and every business seminar you attend, commit to taking away a minimum of three things from each effort. You can certainly take away more, but commit to three at the very least.

Humility is the key here.

Here is the **Try it...Apply it...Fry it** approach to reading this book:

Try It

- Identify a business **Tool** you want to investigate.
- Try it for 30 days in a variety of situations.

This duration will give you an accurate read on worthiness.

Apply It

- If it passes muster, then plan on adding it to your business.
- To apply it, make it an operational procedure.

Fry It

- If it doesn't work for you, then fry it (remove it).

Ultimately, this book provides a **Tool Chest** of tested and proven business ingredients. Picking and choosing what you want to try will be the fun part.

You will find that **Improvement** is central to most of the great business people who came before us. The **Try it…Apply it…Fry it** approach will help facilitate your professional growth and improve your business.

Guardrails
The Tools

The following information will protect and guide your business. It will conserve your money and deliver results. Etch it on your minds, and incorporate it into the recipe for your business.

I'll start with an analogy. Analogies are powerful because they enable us to take something complicated and make it easy to understand. Baked into this manuscript are three analogies designed to simplify and organize the enclosed information.

The first analogy I present is the eight-drawer **Tool Chest**. Every time you think of this book, just picture walking into a garage and seeing that red and silver mechanics **Tool Chest** with eight drawers. When you need something to help you, just as if you were looking for a screwdriver, you go the chest and open the appropriate drawer (**Customer**, **Service**, **Money**, etc.) and look for the **Tool** or **Tools** you need.

The second analogy is this:

- Your business is like a car.
- Operating your business is like driving your car.
- You are driving on the highway to a destination.
- A steep drop threatens to the left of the highway.
- A sheer cliff intimidates to the right.
- **Guardrails** protect your car from veering off the road.

The image we draw is driving down this highway where trouble is to our left and right. Thankfully our driving lane is protected on both sides by **Guardrails**. These lifesaving installations are designed to keep us on a straight path toward our eventual destination: satisfied customers. We want to remain safe on the road and continue the journey.

The various **Tools** in this book are your **Guardrails**. Protecting your business from danger, from consistently losing customers and possibly going out of business are central themes of this book. Assisting in your company health, growth and development are benefits the **Guardrails** will provide.

Silent Business Killer

In the late 1980s, I came across a study by the Technical Assistance Research Program (1985). The findings floored me, and the immediate impact was as powerful that day as it is now. The results revealed:

- 26 of 27 customers fail to report bad experiences.
- This reason is they expect no satisfaction by complaining.
- 91% of those who don't complain won't come back.
- The average upset consumer tells nine to ten colleagues.
- 13% of the malcontents spread the news to 20 or more people.

Expecting no action if they do complain, most unhappy customers disappear and never come back. In the process, they share their negative experience with many people and make a healthy future difficult for the poorly performing company.

If this is your company, the underlying takeaway is that if you are not making customers happy, these unhappy people join a powerful, behind-the-scenes force that diminishes your business success without your ever knowing or hearing about it. Understanding this is what I consider to be the *Secret Sauce* of this book.

I label this the "Silent Business Killer" or the **SBK** effect. The phenomenon destroys businesses. The **SBK** lurks everywhere and has an eternal battery that never stops working against you.

What became crystal clear was that all of this happens sight unseen. The negatively affected business rarely knows that this customer/potential customer cancer is taking root and doing damage. Time and again I have witnessed business problems and issues that can be connected to the **SBK**.

Analogy number three is this:

- The steep drop to the left of the highway is the **SBK**.
- The sheer cliff to the right of the highway is lost customers.
- Stay on the road in pursuit of satisfied customers.

You won't hear or read this anywhere else. I have never witnessed corporate leadership mention anything about this quiet, sneaky and destructive force. **Why?** Because in most cases the negative experiences are unseen, unheard, not tracked and not measured by companies. The **SBK** operates in the shadows and very rarely speaks out, yet the negative impact is a powerful force. The underlying cause is really the vital message to all the readers of this book. When the **SBK** strikes, it is most often directly connected to something your company is doing incorrectly or not doing. Repeated strikes lead to loss of business. The disappearance of a customer is not likely occurring because of outside, coincidental forces.

SimpleBiz360™ is built on these three analogies:

1) The book is an eight-drawer **Tool Chest**.
2) Business **Guardrails** are the **Tools** in this book.
3) Satisfied customers are the result of avoiding **SBKs**.

The Lost Customer

One-person companies encounter challenging costs whenever faced with finding new customers to replace lost ones. The excessive expenses associated with client prospecting can cripple solopreneurs who must stop forward motion, go backwards and scramble to reinvent a paying consumer. This stifles productivity, growth, profitability, progress and enthusiasm.

A lost customer usually gets tangled up with some form of the **SBK** effect before they fall off the edge never to return. Of course, this is not always the case as some consumers depart for reasons unrelated to the dreaded **SBK**. I am passionate about preventing the loss of a customer. I am equally enticed by identifying what promotes the customer defection and doing everything I can to protect against that outcome.

I once worked for a company that constantly lost customers after one or two transactions. All that hard work to obtain the customer was quickly negated with their departure due to poor service from us. Over and over this happened.

I did everything in my power, but I could not correct the internal mess that led to the loss of hard-earned clients. Lies, embellishments, promises broken, false test reports, more lies, and unapproved product substitutions — you name it, and it happened. The majority of customers left and never came back for seconds. I was constantly replacing lost customers. I was spinning my wheels. Ownership dismissed most of my observations and showed little interest in correcting the issues.

As an individual business owner, you have the ability to avoid these disaster stories. You can write a script and perform in ways that lead to customer retention with **Repeat Customers**. Some business models don't support the **Repeat Customer**, but they rely on happy customers leading to **Referral Customers**. Some business models blend both the **Repeat & Referral Customer** types.

The Repeat Customer

Let's say you run a lawn maintenance business. Your goal is to make Mr. and Mrs. Smith so happy with your work that they invite you to provide service next year from mid-March through mid-November.

The Smiths sign up for the season, and you service their lawn every ten days for $45.00 per lawn cutting. That's $990.00 of revenue (22 lawn cuttings) per year from the Smiths. However, if you suffer an **SBK** strike, then you have to find a new customer to replace that steady, $990.00 annual customer. That customer loss becomes very expensive to replace.

The **Repeat Customer** format has an annuity aspect to it. In other words, you can count on them to order in the same pattern next month or next year, and that business pattern becomes a stable part of your future earnings, provided they don't depart for some reason. This reorder rhythm can be charted in dollars and used in your monthly and annual projections.

Let's say in 2017 your lawn maintenance company had 15 seasonal customers at $990.00 per season. This is $14,850 in revenue for lawn cutting. Factoring in a couple of customers leaving (one moves, the other has a family member take over yard work), you can safely report a minimum 2018 projection to your accountant (without growth) of $12,870.

Simply explained, if you have 15 customers this year and you keep 13 of them next year, you have an 87% retention rate or 13% loss (attrition) of customers. Let's say every year you get 15 new customers but lose two of them to attrition. In year two, you have

26 customers, and in year three you have 39, etc. This is solid customer retention and allows you to grow **Repeat** business nicely.

If this is like your business model, this is a great position to be in. Keep avoiding SBKs, and keep your eye on earning that **Repeat Customer**.

When you let the SBK hit, you lose many more than two customers per year. This makes it hard to grow and enjoy owning your business. You become like the mouse on a wheel...you are constantly spinning around going nowhere. When you see retention rates of less than 50%, it is safe to say that the SBK is striking you often. The cost to re-invent those lost customers will take a heavy toll on you, your bill paying, your enthusiasm and your business reputation.

The Referral Customer

If you run a one-and-done business, then you have to create a **Referral** playbook and game plan. In other words, you enable your happy, one-time customer to assist you in obtaining new clients. Some of you (like the lawn maintenance business) will have a blend of the two business models.

If this is your business model (deck builder, wedding planner, interior designer, house painter, etc.), then you want to ensure your jobs are done exceptionally well so that you can gain the **Referral Customer**. This is where you must steer 180 degrees in the opposite direction of the SBK. Rather than have people sinking your ship at the backyard barbecue, you want them giving out your cell phone number because you do good work.

The Repeat/Referral Customer

Let's look at a blended business model. In 2018, you project 26 customers for lawn maintenance after picking up 15 **Referral Customers** and losing two for the second straight year. Now you have 26 seasonal customers and are looking at $25,740 in revenue to start 2018. Let's say the trend continues and 2019 brings 15 new customers and two lost customers. Now in 2019, there are 39 seasonal customers at $38,610 in business. This is what a healthy **Repeat/Referral Blended** business model can look like.

When the forces of the **SBK** work against you, sustaining your business becomes difficult. Avoiding the **SBK** creates satisfied clients that assist in the growth and longevity of your company. The obvious annual goal is to continue to fill your calendar, while obtaining larger and higher paying jobs in the future.

Please imprint the following on your mind:

- Many **SBK** strikes result from what we do wrong.
- Many **SBK** strikes result from what we *fail* to do.

Summary

SimpleBiz360™ and the hundreds of **Timeless Business Tools** will assist you in running healthy, customer-pleasing businesses. Nothing fancy! The **Guardrails (Tools)** will prove to be powerful and effective for your journey. Stay in your lane between the rails, and benefit from growth-oriented forward motion.

These 255 **Tools** will be individually explored in future podcasts. The goal is to spend 10-15 minutes on each **Tool** and feature examples, stories and honest discussion designed to help you improve your business skills and company. We will also offer basic and affordable services that provide direct input to your company. Please visit **www.simplebiz360.com** for more information about the podcast schedule and additional services.

I hope you find this book to be easy on the mind and quick on the eyes. In the end, my sincere hope is that *SimpleBiz360*™ will assist you with the following:

1) Discover more enjoyment in small business ownership.
2) Retain more of your hard-earned profits.
3) Get a better return on your investment of time and money.

Enjoy owning and operating your business. I hope your dreams come true and that you can work for yourself the remainder of your business career.

Thank you for the opportunity to assist you in the fun and fascinating world of business. I am honored that you purchased *SimpleBiz360*™.

Identify, communicate and deliver
customer-focused EXPECTATIONS
that create strong relationships and
provide high-quality transactions.

TOOLS 1–28

Since 1989 I have played "detective" with business situations. What works? What fails? How can success be repeated? How can best practices be transferred from one industry to another? How can I learn from past mistakes and avoid them in the future? What business conduct is unique to pleasing customers? What can I do to stand out among my competitors?

Along this path I bumped into learning more about **EXPECTATIONS.** Strangely I discovered that many business operation issues are directly connected to poorly communicated **EXPECTATIONS,** or the lack of **EXPECTATIONS** altogether.

The second truth I encountered is that poor **EXPECTATIONS** lead to costly "clean up" time. The amount of energy I currently devote to problem solving seems to be much higher than ten years ago. Many of these situations are rooted in poor **EXPECTATIONS.** This can be dangerously costly to the self-employed. Issue resolution and back-pedaling happen way too often. Stopping forward motion and going backwards to fix problems presents obstacles to success.

SimpleBiz360™ is devoted to ways that prevent costly back-pedaling and set quality **EXPECTATIONS** that lead to consistent forward motion, customer-pleasing programs and satisfied customers.

First Things First

The customer will always write your story for you. From their initial transaction to all their repetitive purchases and referrals, they will be the judge and jury. Trusting that, make your best attempt to follow these suggestions to facilitate customer retention, referrals and overall company improvement:

- Sit in the customer chair.
- See through customer glasses.
- Understand customer perceptions of your company.
- Buy your own products to experience being the customer.

My initial suggestion is that you find a favorite quiet place to contemplate business uninterrupted. Maybe you choose a beach, a park or a quiet room with a comfortable chair. Wherever you go, turn off all phones, music and electronics. Have a notepad and pen with you. Isolate yourself and focus. Simply think and jot down your thoughts without distractions.

Ask yourself hard questions about the customer experience:

- Imagine you are buying or using your own product.
- Write down observations to your thoughts and questions.
- What do you like about your products and company?
- What don't you like about your offerings?
- What would you change about the way you do business?
- Are you pleasing customers during the transaction process?
- Do you know if customers are generally satisfied?
- Do you demonstrate care and respect for customers?

This ongoing exercise will prove to be beneficial.

Consult your notes to help you figure all this out, then bake these concepts into your business model. These will become a set of reliable and consistent customer **EXPECTATIONS** that will lead to obtaining, keeping and growing quality clients while minimizing costly back-pedaling time.

Customer Focus

This is where many companies fall short and lose consumers to the competition. Solopreneurs and small business owners must achieve comprehending what a potential business transaction will look like and feel like to a client. This knowledge will serve as a powerful foundation for how you handle your day-to-day operations. Thoroughly understanding the customer perspective will lead to **Repeat** and/or **Referral** business.

Deck Building Example

I'm not picking on deck builders in the next example, but I need something to work with here. This home improvement project scenario will illustrate setting quality **EXPECTATIONS**:

- You, the homeowner, call ten deck builders.
- Two of them return your call.
- Both contractors agree to meet you on a certain day and time.
- Only one shows up at your house on time for the meeting.
- This individual surveys the job and quotes $5,000.
- The company is moderately rated, bonded and insured.
- Agreed completion date is 25 days (for big family reunion).
- Both parties agree to the price and completion date.
- You make down payment ($1,500) to finance the materials.
- On day 15, the second $1,500 installment is due.
- The balance is due upon completion.
- The target start date is two days from your meeting date.
- The deck builder will call tomorrow to confirm start date.

Now the fun starts. The **X** represents irritating business conduct.

X Tomorrow comes and you don't get a call.
X Two days later, no one shows up.
X The cell phone voicemail is full.
X The office phone goes directly to voicemail.
X You leave daily messages on voicemail.
X Repeated emails go unanswered.
X Three, four, five days go by…nothing!

Then on the morning of the sixth day, who comes pulling up in your driveway at 8:15 a.m. as you are backing out of the garage to go to work? You guessed it! You bite your lip, see all the wood on the truck, and you are elated the project is starting. You ask no questions for fear of upsetting the contractor. Semi-regretting you didn't lambast the deck builder for blatant unprofessionalism, you try to calm yourself down in the car. You switch from morning radio talk shows to the soothing serenade of classical music on your 15-minute commute.

Feeling relieved, you then decide to go home for lunch to see the progress.

X You pull up and see no truck or string markings in the yard.
X All you see is lumber dumped off to the side of the driveway.
• You eat lunch, stay a few extra minutes but see no one.
• You go back to work.
X You come home to find the wood has not been moved.
X You realize that no deck builder ever came back.

Six weeks later, your deck is finished, but it is two weeks *after* the big family reunion. You are now thoroughly stressed out and fatigued from 42 days of agonizing guesswork about the project and completion date. Summer is more than half over, and you sort of wish fall would get here quickly. Your brother heavily criticizes you in front of the entire family for not managing your deck builder well. If it was his house, he would read the contractor the riot act and short pay by $500 for not completing it in 25 days. Your mother chimes in by apologizing to the entire family for your inability to get the deck ready in time. She finishes off by boldly broadcasting that she wishes the reunion was at her house.

For the next year, every time you look at the deck it dredges up the bad memories. Your mother brings this story up at almost every family get-together and holiday gathering for the rest of her life. All this because of a deck!

Sound familiar? Oh yeah…you know it does. Dozens of people will read this and think I was snooping on them because it happened to them with eerie similarity. I too have experienced this type of nightmare with one deck I had built. To all you deck builders: I also had two others constructed with absolute professionalism and timeliness. Thank you!

What If?

Okay…let's park here. The deck builder probably has no idea that this project has had such a long-lasting ripple effect on this family. **This story illuminates real money-losing possibilities for contractors or companies that don't look and see reality through customer eyeglasses.**

What if this story had different components? What if this contractor embraced **Customer Focus** and approached the deck building business through the eyes of the customer? What if this contractor (1) created an **Expectation Path**, (2) told the customer about it and then (3) followed the path? What if this contractor engaged the customer along the way?

Based on what I have been taught, what I have experienced and what I do myself, here is my professional suggestion on how to inject customer-pleasing and money-making **EXPECTATIONS** into the equation.

Customer Focus Example

DECK BUILDER: "Well Mr. and Mrs. Jones, I appreciate this opportunity to quote you this job. Based on all of your criteria, I am committing to do this job within the 21–25 days needed. The cost I have arrived at is $5,000. However, before I present this simple agreement to you for your authorization, I would like to share something with you that is near and dear to me. I call it my **Expectation List**. It is designed for my customers, and it sets me apart from my competitors.

"I include a copy in the agreement. Here is a printed copy for you to look at while I run down the list. Please stop me if you have any questions."

Example Expectation List

- ✓ Carry 20–25 copies of your list with you at all times.
- ✓ Laminate one copy for presentations.

Communication
- My cell phone is the best way to reach me (1-SSS-BBB-3600).
- Call or text me.
- Office voicemail (1-360-JJJ-MMMM) is checked once per day.
- Return calls are made within 24 hours.
- On the job cell calls are limited to family and suppliers.
- Customer return calls are made during lunch hour.
- My current email address is: info@simplebiz360.com.
- I return all emails within 24 hours.
- Communication is polite, professional and integrity-driven.

Jobsite
- Arrival time is between 8:00 a.m. and 9:00 a.m. each day.
- My jobsite departure time is 4:30–5:00 p.m.
- Jobsite will be cleaned 30 minutes prior to departure.
- I take a 15-minute break in the morning.
- Public restroom is visited during 15-minute break.
- Lunch break (non-working hour) is 12:00 noon–1:00 p.m.
- I may or may not leave during lunch.
- Lunch will be shortened if early departure is required.
- I text any deviation to arrival/departure/break times.
- All homeowner doors are promptly closed behind me.
- I appreciate secured family pets during my work hours.
- Completion dates are kept (provided weather cooperates).

Materials & Specifications

- Materials are purchased before 9:00 a.m. or after 5:00 p.m.
- I inventory common nails, screws and fasteners.
- Deviations in materials require your approval.
- Deviations with specifications require your approval.
- Material changes may result in cost changes.
- Receipts will be supplied for any cost deviations.

Job Conclusion/Jobsite Pictures

- 360° job inspection is conducted at conclusion.
- Balance (33%) is due after owner inspection and approval.
- I ask permission to take jobsite pictures after completion.
- I ask permission to use photos (minus home/email addresses).

Reference & Referral Award

- References & Referrals help to grow my business.
- If satisfied, feel free to write an email or letter.
- I ask your permission to use these for my business portfolio.
- All email and street addresses will be scrubbed.
- Reference/Referral partners are eligible for $100 gift card.
- Gift cards are awarded upon completion of referral jobs.
- $100 gift cards are issued for local dining establishments.

Post Job Inspection

- I schedule 360° jobsite inspection at 180-days post completion.
- I schedule 360° jobsite inspection at 365-days post completion.
- Materials/craftsmanship defects are covered by my company.

Hmmm...

Imagine...

...if this contractor delivered on the **Expectation Path** they built?
...how different the family reunion might have been?
...how this **Expectation List** would be talked about?
...how many word-of-mouth referral customers would call?
...what the contractor's future calendar would look like?
...the possible financial security achieved from this conduct?
...the potential for expansion and growth?

Consider the following very carefully!

With regards to deck building, *quality, price* and *craftsmanship* are more or less a given among all the competitors. Those business tenants are simply the price of admission. Let's be honest, if you are going to make your living building decks, you are probably relatively good at it. When all is said and done, if we compared the craftsmanship of three deck building companies, the naked eye of most homeowners would not be able to see many differences. The same would go for all home improvement professionals, like bathroom remodelers, floor and carpet installers, house painters, kitchen remodelers and electricians.

What the homeowner deserves is *quality, price* and *craftsmanship*. These deliverables are expected by paying consumers and necessary for any home improvement company to compete.

Question: What is the elephant in the room?
Answer: What customers don't want!

Assuming *quality, price* and *craftsmanship* are equal among the competing contractors, here is what homeowners DON'T want:

Ø Unreliable arrival & departure times.
Ø Mysterious and unexplained jobsite departures.
Ø Short work days.
Ø Unreturned phone/text/email messages.
Ø Messy end-of-day jobsites (that homeowners have to clean).
Ø Outside doors left open for long periods of time.
Ø Escaped pets (usually from unsecured doors and gates).
Ø Excessive bugs in the house.
Ø Tools not put away at the end of workday.
Ø Ladders not put away.
Ø Nails in the driveway.
Ø Contractor purchasing materials during job time.
Ø Contractor forgetting essential tools.
Ø Missed deadlines.

When you deliver what customers deserve, need and want, combined with addressing what they *don't* want, you have a recipe for success. Careful consideration for customer perspective will help lead to long and gainful self-employment.

This approach oozes of professionalism and creates a steady diet of potential clients who will pay top dollar for your services. Again, and extremely important, you have to create customer-focused **EXPECTATIONS** and deliver on them.

Sam Walton knew this to be true when he crafted Rule #8 of "Sam's Rules for Building a Business" in *SAM WALTON Made in America*: "Exceed your customers' expectations. If you do, they'll come back over and over" (1992).

Here is bad news and good news. The bad news is that after decades of declining customer service performance, many consumers don't expect good service. This is a classic **SBK**. Consequently, if you succeed in surpassing customer **EXPECTATIONS**, your business will be viewed as shockingly fresh. This different approach will be viewed favorably and will contribute to business sustainability and growth.

Most issues are the result of **unclear** or **unstated EXPECTATIONS**:

- "I thought it came in a box."
- "I didn't know it was disassembled."
- "You never told me it was this thin."
- "Your website says assembly is easy…not 22 steps."
- "The directions are very confusing."
- "You never told me delivery is two to four weeks."
- "Nobody called to tell me delivery is delayed by four weeks."
- "My credit card was charged but the order never shipped."
- "I never approved this color."
- "Why did you do the repair for $150 without calling me?"
- "I thought you were installing 6" gutters…not small ones."
- "Your menu doesn't mention peanut sauce… I'm allergic."

When the issues are minor, you could lose a customer and have a small refund to deal with. As the products, services, transactions and customers become larger, the issue resolution can be financially crippling. In addition, you open yourself up to the dangers enveloped in customer perception.

Perception IS reality. We will talk more about this later in the next chapters and in some podcasts.

The business book *Raving Fans* addresses the need for consistency with **EXPECTATIONS**: "The worst thing you can do is meet expectations one time, fall short another and exceed every now and then. I guarantee you'll drive your customer nuts and into the hands of the competition first chance they get" (Blanchard & Bowles, 1993).

Expectation "Briefers"

Definition of a briefer: A short ditty, or brief story pertaining to a business situation.

In 1984, Leo J. McDonough (an associate of mine) and I coined this term whenever we would exchange short stories about business situations. I am not sure why, but to this day we have a good chuckle every time either of us says we have a "quick briefer." Thank you, Leo!

I have a couple of funny ones to share with you that happened while writing this book.

BRIEFER #1: While in a hotel room on a recent business trip, a commercial comes on the air and goes something like this:

"Tired of messy contractors? Tired of workers that show up whenever they want or leave without telling you? Stop dealing with them and start dealing with the SB360 Company. We show up every day, we are on time and leave no mess behind!"

Cha-Ching! Simple **EXPECTATIONS** that recognize perception through customer eyes!

BRIEFER #2: While recently interacting with an attorney who was recommended to me, I get his voice message that goes something like this:

"We are sorry we cannot answer the phone right now. However, we realize your call is important. Our reliable policy is to call you back within 24 hours. Our call back hours are from 11:00 a.m. to 12 noon and again from 4:00 p.m. to 5:00 p.m. every day. We thank you for your inquiry."

I applauded him with praise as I left my message and again when he called me back at 4:08 that afternoon. The attorney told me his firm takes prompt call-backs very seriously.

Cha-Ching! Simple **EXPECTATIONS** that recognize perception through customer eyes!

EXPECTATION TOOLS 1–28

Determine what customers:

1. **WANT**.
2. **NEED**.
3. **DESERVE**.
4. DO *NOT* WANT.

5. Create your **INTERNAL EXPECTATION** list.
6. Write a **CUSTOMER EXPECTATION** list.
7. **COMMUNICATE** Customer Expectation List to clients.
8. **CARRY** print copies of your Customer Expectation List.
9. **LAMINATE** and carry your Customer Expectation List.
10. **DISPLAY** customer expectations on your company website.
11. **MEET** or exceed your stated customer expectations.
12. Communicate **COMPLETION/DELIVERY** dates.
13. Provide voluntary **UPDATES** on completion/delivery.
14. Create **REALISTIC** completion/delivery dates.
15. **DEFINE** product and service programs clearly.
16. Provide detail in product **DESCRIPTIONS**.
17. Include **SPECIFICATIONS** in product descriptions.
18. Publish clear **WARRANTY** guidelines.
19. Explain **RETURN** policies.
20. Outline processes with step-by-step **DETAIL**.
21. Use **SIMPLE** words in all explanations.
22. **REFLECT** on good and bad customer interactions.
23. Ask customers for their **EXPECTATIONS**.
24. Communicate **IMPROVEMENTS** to your customers.
25. Obtain customer **FEEDBACK**.

Notify customers of your turnaround time for:

26. **RETURN** phone calls.
27. **RETURN** emails.
28. **UPDATES**.

"Every brand has at its core a
substance that gives it strength.
You have to understand it before you grow it."

Scott Bedbury — *A New Brand World* (2002)

TOOLS 29–62

SBK = Silent Business Killer

What is your professional center point? What are the primary character traits that make you unique? In other words, what is at the **CORE** of who you are and what you do as a business person?

If you had to pinpoint the exact middle of what your company does, what is that epicenter? When you answer these self-imposed questions, you will be face-to-face with your brand identity. In the world of solopreneurs, the one-person entity becomes the brand! Customers and potential customers will associate you with your company. You and your brand are blended into one mix that draws strength, creativity and profitability from the **CORE** of who you are and what you do. As a result, you owe it to yourself, your business, your investment, your family and your customers to accomplish two essential tasks:

1. Create and operate with unshakeable **Core Values.**
2. Build upon your professional **Core Competencies**.

These ethics and abilities will be central to everything you do now and in the future. Handled correctly, these operational components will enhance your brand and business. Handled incorrectly, these bedrock elements will tarnish your brand, complicate your business and possibly destroy it altogether.

Core Values

Core Values set the long-term foundation of your business identity. They put stakes in the ground to establish who you are as an owner-operator and as a company. These stated values are closely related to expectations. These values become the glue that binds all of your business ingredients and operational expectations together. Moreover, living up to these values is crucial. Customers will hold you accountable if you don't deliver on these cornerstone business ingredients. In addition, you need to hold yourself accountable. Be careful…if you casually throw these values around in writing or discussions, then do the opposite, hypocrisy will be your calling card and the door opens wide for **SBKs**.

My personal **Core Values** are very near and dear to me. I put elements of my company **Core Values** in my sales agency tagline which reads: *Solutions. Performance. Integrity.* This **Core Value** tagline has bolstered my reputation and assisted me out of a few minor business situations where customers questioned my integrity. The total sum of all my **Core Values** is **Professionalism.** This is my calling card. I want my business tombstone to read, "Here lies a true professional." I have written my **Core Values** on an 8.5" x 11" sheet of paper and give it to customers. I entitled the sheet "Professionalism," and I open with the following introduction:

From 1984 to 1987 I was fortunate to work in the Wall Street area of New York City. I called on headquarters of worldwide banks, brokerage houses, insurance companies and large Wall Street law firms. I conducted daily business with CEOs, EVPs, SVPs, VPs, GMs, Senior Partners, Partners and Administrators.

Early in my career I began to ask these successful executives what advice they could give me to assist in my success and personal business development.

Three years and many suggestions later, the advice I most often received was: Be professional.

Define "professionalism" the way you want. My choice is to define it with my personal list of **Core Values**. They are as follows.

CORE VALUE TOOLS 29–47

Operate with:

29: **INTEGRITY.**
30: **HONESTY.**
31: **CONSISTENCY.**
32: **RELIABILITY.**
33: **RESPECT.**
34. **COURTESY.**
35. **POLITENESS.**
36: **KINDNESS.**
37: **PUNCTUALITY.**
38: **THOROUGHNESS.**
39: **ATTENTION-TO-DETAIL.**
40: **APPROPRIATENESS.**
41: **DEPENDABILITY.**
42: **ACCURACY.**
43: **SINCERITY.**
44: **HUMILITY.**
45: **PRODUCT KNOWLEDGE.**
46. **CLEANLINESS.**
47: Good **HYGIENE.**

If price, quality and delivery are equal among all competitors, **Tools #29–47** win every time. If not in the short term, for sure in the long run. Should you want to maximize your efforts in obtaining new customers, these **Tools** will help you obtain **Repeat** business, **Referrals** and a full work schedule.

Trust me…if you endorse and use **Tools #29–47**, your head will never hit the pillow at night not knowing what you are doing tomorrow. Your plate will be full.

The key is that these must be *unshakeable*. Cement them into your business. Don't plant in dirt or sand! Make these permanent, and they will lead to a healthy brand representation.

The success of many large companies can also be connected to the daily adherence to **Core Values.** Consider the perspective from one of the initial giants of the technology age in Buck Rodgers' *The IBM Way* (1986):

"IBM'S greatness has been built on some very simple ideas and principles. Nothing very complicated or profound—little things that, I hope are still being taught to children by their parents, teachers and religious leaders. Things like thoughtfulness, courtesy and integrity."

Core Competency

What are you best at? Chances are you started the business because of a strong self-confidence in your area of service or product expertise. This primary excellence is your **Core Competency** and should be the centerpiece of your company. Your brand and professional identity are directly tied to your abilities.

Continue to feature your best skill set as your "hallmark." What are you known for? Remember, your **Core Competency** got you started, and most likely, this area of expertise will ride off into the sunset with you. I am not suggesting you never layer other products or services on top of your best skill. Create a framework of this concept by drawing a circle and putting your best skill in the middle. The center is your bread and butter. The goods and services you supply should be in close proximity to the center point **Core Competency**. Straying too far away from your best skill set can be costly and dangerous.

The investment you made to start your business has money, time and sweat equity laced throughout the history of your company. Ensure that you get a great return on your investment, and give yourself a chance to enjoy business ownership until retirement. You maximize your chances of doing that by operating with unshakeable **Core Values** and continual focus on your **Core Competencies**.

You are the company. You are the brand. The brand "buck" starts and stops with you. I urge you to improve on and continue to become the best at what you are good at. Build and strengthen your brand from the **CORE**.

CORE COMPETENCY TOOLS 48–62

Do the following with your **Core Competency** (CC):

48. **IDENTIFY.**
49. **PROMOTE.**
50. **POLISH** (Improve/Enhance).
51. Provide **PROOF.**
52. Obtain **TESTIMONIALS.**
53. Establish **REWARDS** for customers who buy your CC.
54. **VALUE** CC with your best time and effort.
55. **REDUCE** CC costs (over time).
56. **INCREASE** the profitability of CC through efficiencies.
57. Continually **MEASURE** the costs of your CC.
58. Know how your **COMPETITION** markets your CC.
59. Identify and market CC **UNIQUENESS.**
60. **COMMUNICATE** your CC uniqueness to customers.
61. **EXPAND** your business around CC as the centerpiece.
62. Establish your core **HALLMARK** and live up to it.

"The more you solve customer's
problems, the more business you'll get."

Mitzi Perdue
"Frank Perdue's Lessons"
Tough Man, Tender Chicken,
Business & Life Lessons from Frank Perdue
(2015)

TOOLS 63–94

SBK = Silent Business Killer

I learned a number of unforgettable rules when I joined Lanier Business Products at the beginning of my career.

Rule #1: CUSTOMERS buy from people they like.
Rule #2: Think of the CUSTOMERS first, last and always.

In other words, the CUSTOMER is the center of everything we do. It is through their consumer lenses that our goods and services should be designed, developed, provided and followed up on.

Winning the Middle

Not all people will like you, nor will they buy from you. You will never know all the reasons for buying decisions, and some reasons would shock you. The key for the solopreneur and small business owner is to try and ensure you **Win the Middle**. In other words, don't present yourself in a way where the buyer sees you as an "either/or" proposition. You want to avoid putting the client in a position to determine whether you are either liked or disliked. Rather, conduct yourself in a manner where the potential consumer sees you in the middle where you are defined as a professional. This enables the decision maker to start liking you.

Gregarious, "type A" personalities that boast and project arrogance in place of confidence have difficulty winning the middle. Robotic, unemotional and unenthusiastic people also have difficulty with the middle. Professionalism safeguards against the "either/or" situation and allows you to proceed with earning the trust of the CUSTOMER.

Likes/Dislikes

Common sense plays a huge role here. I don't have the crystal ball with all the answers. However, I do have decades of witnessing and observing **CUSTOMER** tendencies towards vendor satisfaction or dissatisfaction.

Much of what **CUSTOMERS** like can be connected to the adherence of quality **Core Value Tools**. These **Tools** address those interests central to a **CUSTOMER** liking you and trusting you. What decision makers disapprove can be detected with keen observation and listening, yet any business person can easily gloss over these points of irritation.

For example, lies, boasting, arrogance, blame shifting and an argumentative demeanor will not get **CUSTOMERS** to like you. Neither will consistent unreturned phone calls and unreturned email as they are indications that you service buyers when it is convenient for you. Buyers tend to be turned off if they know your company flies that self-centered flag. The **SBK** effect will subtly creep into those business models that are not in touch with consumer desires.

What pleases or irritates customers are wonderful perspectives to mull over in your quiet spaces when you have a notepad handy and you can improve on your **Expectations** and **Core Values**. Carefully contemplate what happened on previous jobs when you were consistently late, didn't show up at all, wasted time, changed your fees mid-stream or missed completion dates. My educated guess is that you will discover the **SBK** came calling and led to some **CUSTOMER** defections.

The Centerpiece

Frank Perdue understood putting customers at the center of his business efforts. According to Ted Cook, one of the early marketing reps at Perdue Farms, Inc., "Frank wanted us to keep in mind that, 'The buyer has plenty of headaches, and our job is to make sure that we aren't one of them. The more we solve his problems, the more business we'll get'" (Perdue, 2015).

"Each customer counts" was another lesson from Mr. Perdue. This is an attitude that came from the top and flowed throughout the organization to all 19,000 employees. Imagine how our clients would feel if we treated each and every one importantly, regardless of their revenue generation or prestige?

Commenting on Frank Perdue's leadership style, former Perdue Farms President, Bob Turley, adds, "He always knew what customers wanted, and a lot of that was because he was out there listening. One of his greatest statements was, 'To be successful we must develop products and services for the consumers before they realize it is something they want'" (Perdue, 2015).

Keep reminding yourself of the following:

A. Make **CUSTOMERS** the center of all you do.
B. Demonstrate respect for your clients continually.
C. Rely on **Core Values** for operational guidance.
D. Set realistic, customer-pleasing **Expectations**.
E. Earn **Repeat** and/or **Referral Customers**.

Pleasing clients requires a dedicated commitment to putting them first. You get closer to excellence and long-term sustainability each time products and services are modified with enhanced benefits for **Customers**. Try viewing the consumer like the ball in a tennis match. I'm oversimplifying a beautiful sport, but keep your eye on the ball and the score will take care of itself.

Leaders from The Forum Corporation and Wal-Mart explain the value of customer-centric business conduct in the following excerpts:

"Forum research found, to no one's surprise, that the companies making real progress in serving their customers are led by people who themselves put the customer first. More than that, they believe passionately in giving the customer what he or she wants."

Richard C. Whiteley — The Forum Corporation's
The Customer Driven Company (1991)

"For my whole career in retail, I have stuck by one principle. It's a simple one, and I repeated it over and over and over in this book until I'm sure you're sick to death of it. But, I'm going to say it again anyway: The secret of success retailing is to give your customers what they want."

Sam Walton with John Huey
SAM WALTON Made in America (1992)

Perception <u>IS</u> Reality

In my opinion, **CUSTOMER** perception seems to be largely ignored by many companies. As society changes decade by decade, facts seem to be giving way to personal opinion. Consumers weigh and measure products and services differently than even 20 years ago. In my opinion, in 2019 **CUSTOMER Perception IS Reality**. You must be conscientious of this as you conduct business. If you miss this point, you are already in danger of having your company fail. Seriously...I firmly believe we have arrived at this juncture. This is bad!

What this suggests is that more than ever, companies have to limit mistakes to ensure high-quality transactions resulting in healthy **CUSTOMER** perceptions. First impressions are now more important than ever. Remember the old cliché, "You only get one chance at a first impression."

The first contact about this book with a publishing house was a horrible experience. There were all kinds of surrounding noises and people talking in the background. My contact seemed preoccupied, had a hard time finding words and could hardly string a full sentence together. Seriously! Then it seemed the person shifted to a script as the dialogue smoothed out a tiny bit. Sadly, this person was so absorbed in what they had to say next that they did not listen to what I was saying.

Immediately I thought, "I need to end this conversation fast because there is no way that I am handing over a 30-year project to this person. No way!" Ironically, their publishing program actually looked good when I reviewed it on their website. However, my first 60 seconds was a disaster, and by the 61st second it became apparent that they were not getting one penny of my business. Period. Paragraph. End of story! Every bone of my body urges you to embrace this factor: **Perception IS Reality.**

Customer Types

CUSTOMER types can be simplified into three categories for most business models:

1) **Repeat** (annuity)
2) **Referral** (project)
3) **Repeat/Referral** (blend of annuity and project)

We outlined these three buying profiles in the introduction, and we will look at them here from another angle. Consider these key points:

- Earning satisfied customers is essential.
- Receiving future business from happy clients is necessary.
- Retaining customers is a low cost/high reward formula.
- Minimizing customer loss is critical (you will lose clients).
- Understanding causes for dissatisfaction is recommended.
- Correcting bad experience issues delivers long-term benefits.
- Replacing lost clients has a high seek-and-find cost.

Repeat (annuity) purchasing business models are a treasure because they reward good product and service performance with a sturdy growth platform. Like a growing tree, you start with a well planted root system and the branches of new life grow and multiply. Next thing you know, you have a healthy group of first-timers who re-buy over and over, becoming **Repeat** transaction clients that you do not have to find again.

Your costs associated with these re-buy orders keep going down while the profits per order from these **CUSTOMERS** keep going up. **Why?** Simply because you don't have to devote precious time, energy and money to the replacement buyer acquisition process. Once acquired, your mission is to maintain **CUSTOMER** happiness which is usually less time-consuming and less expensive than earning the first order.

The end goal is that you want these **CUSTOMERS** to keep re-ordering because they find value and benefit to the way you conduct business and in your products and services themselves. Overall satisfaction on each transaction is now the clear mission. At a minimum, you must consistently meet their expectations to avoid their defection. Exceeding these expectations will bolster healthy perceptions of your company.

Referral (project-based) Customers make the job of securing future business a little tougher than **Repeat Customers**. The **Referral** business model starts by making a one-and-done **CUSTOMER** happy. In other words, you provide a one-time, mission-specific product or service that cannot be re-bought by that particular client. Some examples of this include home improvement contractors such as fence installers, driveway pavers, deck builders, bathroom or kitchen remodelers and house painters. Other examples are party planners, wedding consultants, website designers and realtors.

Managed correctly, your calendar could be consistently full for the majority of your career. Your goal is to satisfy the **CUSTOMER** to a point where their happiness shuts the door on the **SBKs** and they willingly refer your products and services to other potential clients. What will set you apart are the **Core Values** you adhere to, your keen understanding of **CUSTOMER** relationship principles and avoiding what **CUSTOMERS** don't want.

Repeat/Referral (annuity + project-based) Customers are very common to seasonal or rotational business models. The introduction of this book featured a seasonal lawn maintenance company illustrating this **CUSTOMER** type. Insect control (rotational) is another good example. Technicians may treat homes every four months, so they have a **Repeat** business model. **Referrals** are a big part of business building. When you blend these two, you have this combination **CUSTOMER** type.

Buying vs. Selling

I cut my career teeth in sales, so I could offer substantial elaboration about this subject. However, I realize an enormous portion of solopreneurs and small business owners don't want to be salespeople. Although selling is not for everyone, when you own a business, a buying transaction is a necessity for you to get paid and remain operational.

SimpleBiz360™ is built on the premise that the sales (buying) transaction is the end goal that companies desire. The information in this book is intended to aid and assist small business owners in achieving sales transaction successes by operating their business in ways that are appealing to **CUSTOMERS** and buyers. These appealing actions are the business **Tools** that *SimpleBiz360*™ focuses on.

Companies can develop and use clever marketing. However, if day-to-day business is not conducted in a way that pleases buyers, all the marketing in the world will not deliver **Repeat** transactions or a steady stream of **Referrals**.

SimpleBiz360™ will not focus on selling methods. I am going to address the concept of **Sales** from the angle of **Buying**. I have run into very few people who want to be sold something. Most **CUSTOMERS** feel more comfortable **Buying** goods and services. Purchasing and/or investing makes the decision theirs and not the result of selling techniques.

Of the estimated 20 million solopreneur businesses in the USA, my guess is a small percentage of those companies are owned and operated by current or former sales professionals. The majority of these 20 million companies are likely owned by individuals who have **Core Competencies** they want to use to make a living.

I would be doing you a hefty disservice suggesting your pursuit and mastering of sales techniques is the way for you to achieve your company dreams. If you have a sales background...*GREAT!* If not, I assure you that understanding buying behaviors can be productive for your bank account and genuinely natural for your potential **CUSTOMERS**. It is advantageous for you and your business to understand how **CUSTOMERS**, in most cases, come to their buying decisions.

Various training programs identify the steps of selling and buying. Lanier Business Products taught me this knowledge that I will forever hold in high regard. Here are the **Five Phases of Buying** that **CUSTOMERS** go through on the way to a favorable decision:

ATTENTION: Listening and liking the message and messenger.
INTEREST: Wanting to know more information.
CONVICTION: Realizing this sounds good to them.
DESIRE: Seeing themselves using the products or services.
ACTION: Moving to a favorable decision.

Dining Out and the
Five Steps of Buying

ANALOGY: You send a text message to your friend saying you want to go out and eat tonight. It turns out you passed a billboard for a seafood restaurant that caught your *ATTENTION (1).* That night you drive to this dining establishment, meet your buddy and get seated. The server hands you a menu, reviews specials, and you begin your information gathering to discover what sparks your *INTEREST (2).* In your menu review process, you begin to zero in on the options, and now your *CONVICTION (3)* shifts gears because broiled seafood appeals more to your taste buds than pecan encrusted grouper. Now you start seeing yourself eating the combo assortment over the fish entree. The decision is official...you *DESIRE (4)* the buttery broiled assortment of lobster, flounder, scallops and shrimp. Now the server comes back and asks you what you would like to eat. You respond to the question by taking *ACTION (5)* and selecting the broiled seafood platter with a side salad.

How many times have you gone to a restaurant, progressed through Steps 1, 2, 3 and 4 only to get up and leave when asked for your order? Probably never! **Why?** Because the buying steps 1, 2, 3 and 4 were successfully achieved. The *5th Step (ACTION)* resulted as a natural progression in your decision-making process. The server asked a simple, direct question and your selection completed the transaction. In this example, you (the buyer) have been in control through the entire process.

The same **5-Step Buying Principles** can be applied to your business model. Your potential **CUSTOMERS** will follow this decision-making road map. You don't have to be a salesperson to achieve success in your business. Contrary to popular belief, you don't need to be a good closer to get business. Understanding the **Buying Process** will help you in your efforts. However, just like the server in a restaurant, you need to learn how to ask for the business.

Asking for the Business

This is about as *salesy* as many of you will get. I realize many readers are breaking into a sweat while reading these words. Please trust that I am making this as natural and conversational as possible while delivering proven questions that get the job done. Reality is that most potential **CUSTOMERS** will need to be asked to agree on a transaction. There are two very, very (I stress VERY) simple ways to ask for the business:

Direct Question:
Based on what we discussed, when can we get started on the project?

Alternate Question (either/or):
Would you like me to start on Monday the 12th or will the 19th work better?

These questions are easy on the tongue, easy on the ear and non-confrontational.

IMPORTANT: The anxiety of asking will disappear if you see yourself as the server in the restaurant! These questions fit with the modern SHARING and SHOW-AND-TELL way of doing business. You are showing, telling and asking.

When you are nervous...
REMEMBER THE DINING OUT ANALOGY!

Business Proof

If I had a dollar for every time a salesperson told me they lied to secure a sale, I would probably be able to finance a long weekend stay at a Florida beach condo. I'm not joking! Again...classic **SBKs** at work here!

Many people have become skeptical when it comes to the almighty "sales pitch." Their reasons are valid. This applies to potential **CUSTOMERS** also. Consumers are now conditioned to follow the "buyer beware" mantra as they keenly watch out for the embellishments, or lies. One eyebrow is always up! What is truth? What is fiction?

Buying something is always easier if you can touch it, see it, try it, taste it, smell it or take it for a spin. As you know, not everything can be offered in those formats. Therefore, **CUSTOMERS** are put in a position where they need to believe what the business owner is telling them. Business owners need to get as close to the touch, smell, taste, sight and sound as possible.

Business Proof is a proven approach to bridging the believability gap when all the five senses cannot be exposed to the product. This also helps to make the **Buying Process** more natural and compelling. Without some sort of proof, it is hard for consumers to cut through potential and rampant lies. Before investing in you, **CUSTOMERS** like to be reassured with evidence. They want to know they are making the right decision with their money. Think of the **CUSTOMER** first, last and always…it is their hard-earned money you are asking for!

Business Proof will equip you with simple ways to set yourself and your company apart from this messy little stew of sales pitch lies. By using this reassurance approach, you will establish a reputation for transparency and truthfulness while earning the respect of many **CUSTOMERS**.

I give credit for this to Lanier Business Products. We were taught to compartmentalize and carry this vital and compelling information in an easel-back three-ring binder. Our materials were assembled in an order consistent with this saying: "**EVIDENCE D-E-F-E-A-T-S DISBELIEF**."

EVIDENCE

Demonstrations

Examples

Facts

Exhibits

Analogies

Testimonials

Statistics

DISBELIEF

Today there are various ways to share and communicate this evidence to **CUSTOMERS**.

Laptop, tablet or mobile device presentations can be highly polished and very effective if they work right. Beware! I remember having a very painful meeting with a big, prestigious company where technology failed and the meeting became awkward. Always have a secondary way of salvaging bad technology.

Consider my invitation to go "old school" and make a presentation kit that can be used in place of technology. This kit should contain information that bring facts, truth and track records into the decision-making process of your buyers. A simple and effective way to use this material with potential consumers is by organizing the kit into **Demonstrations, Examples, Facts, Exhibits, Analogies, Testimonials** and **Statistics.** This will help to combat indecision resulting from disbelief in what you say and claim.

Included in the **Business Proof Kit** should be the company **Expectation List, Core Values List**, and **Customer List**. Compile pictures, drawings, spec sheets, flyers, warranty policies, testimonial letters, email copies, certificates, award letters, newspaper articles, magazine articles, blog reviews, web reviews, and other items from the **DEFEATS** categories.

I strongly suggest that you place all this evidence into a large and sturdy three-ring binder that can be easily referenced while working with customers. Utilize page protectors to preserve the information and maintain a professional appearance. Two copies of this kit will be highly beneficial. Keep one in your office and one in your vehicle to ensure you are always prepared. This type of information showcase can be your number one choice for sharing

Business Proof with customers. This three-ring binder can also serve as an effective back-up insurance policy should technology become inoperable in front of customers.

Websites and social media outlets offer effective platforms for showcasing track record information and compelling reassurance material. Just two gentle reminders: Keep social media content zeroed in on business, and avoid opinion. You are 30 seconds from having an opinion go viral, and you may or may not like the outcome.

Personal Business Portfolio

My first sales manager, Morris Asch, recommended that I start assembling my business achievements in a **Personal Business Portfolio**. This was not for bragging rights; it was so I could prove my accomplishments to future employers, banks or investors. I followed his lead and assembled all my information in a three-ring binder.

I have two thick binders and have used them quite often throughout my career. They have made me money, secured consulting jobs and enabled me to stand out as different from other applicants interviewing for the same job.

For example, in 1989 as Director of Sales, Recruiting & Training for a small computer company, a division of the *Wall Street Journal* contacted me about being the feature for a story they were doing on college recruiting and interviewing. American University suggested the magazine talk with me as the institution was impressed with the recruiting program I had put together. Eventually, an article was written and distributed nationally. I have copies of the actual publication and associated correspondence that can prove my skill sets produced this program and resulted in hiring 65 top tier college graduates for entry level sales employment.

You want to be able to share these facts (not stories) at any given opportunity. Be prepared to prove your skill sets and prior work. Indisputable and tangible evidence will bridge the believability gap.

Enthusiasm

I never gave **Enthusiasm** much thought in my early life. Then when I went into my entry level sales position in New York City, the concept of **Genuine Enthusiasm** was introduced to me. Yeah…yeah…okay…in one ear and out the other. I'm energetic, I'm outgoing, and I bound out of bed every morning looking forward to each day as a new adventure. However, focusing on **Enthusiasm** as a standalone concept and business aid? No…not for me!

Well, well…was I in for a shock. Being encouraged to read a business book per month, I started plucking books from my company's Recommended Reading List. I grabbed a timeless manuscript, *How I Raised Myself from Failure to Success in Selling* by Frank Bettger (1947). This was and still is a game changer for me. In fact, I give this book out often. Just last year my son-in-law, a financial advisor, read it. He was amazed at the modern-day relevance and improvement power contained in these thoughts penned over 70 years ago.

In this book, Mr. Bettger explains the essence of how **Enthusiasm** changed him, and I know it can have a changing effect on anyone reading this book.

Powerful Story

In 1907, while making $175 per month, Frank got fired from the Johnstown, Pennsylvania Tri-State League team for laziness. His coach said, *"Whatever you do after you leave here, for heaven's sake, wake yourself up, and put some life and enthusiasm into your work!"*

Then Mr. Bettger got rehired by the Atlantic League in Chester, Pennsylvania for $25 per month. It was there he started to act enthusiastically. He took the advice from his old coach. After just three days of playing in Chester, an old ball player, Danny Meehan, arranged for the New Haven, Connecticut team to give Frank a trial. He made a resolution to be the most enthusiastic player the New England League had ever seen. *"From the minute I appeared on the field, I acted like a man electrified. I acted as though I were alive with a million batteries."*

The newspaper started calling him "PEP" Bettger — the life of the team! His pay went from $25 a month to $185 per month. *"Two years later, two years from the time I was hoping to get $25 a month in that little Chester outfit, I was playing third base for the St. Louis Cardinals and had multiplied my income by thirty times. What did it? Enthusiasm alone did it; nothing but enthusiasm."*

Frank spent two more years on the St. Louis Cardinals before an arm injury prematurely ended his professional baseball career. He transitioned to selling insurance and went on to become one of the most successful insurance sales professionals of his generation. He also blessed audiences by going on the public speaking circuit, telling his story to tens of thousands and inspiring many people to embrace **Genuine Enthusiasm**.

In reading a classic that has stood the test of time, *How To Win Friends & Influence People* by Dale Carnegie, I was floored to read about Charles Schwab (1936). In 1921, Andrew Carnegie paid Charles Schwab a one-million-dollar salary to become the first president of the newly formed United States Steel Company. This was at a time when making a $2,600 annual salary was considered being well-off.

When asked why Charles Schwab thought he was paid that kind of money, he responded:

"I consider my ability to arouse enthusiasm among my people, the greatest asset I possess, and the way to develop the best that is in a person is by appreciation and encouragement."

You may be thinking, "Jeff Mason is lost! How can business examples from the early 1900's have any real applicability in 2019? It is too outdated to be relevant." My answer is that both Frank Bettger and Dale Carnegie harnessed the ability to convey **timeless** and **simple** information in their manuscripts. They offer us sound, perpetually relevant human relations skill sets that can form a strong bedrock of business behavior now and for decades and centuries to come.

Inspired by these classics, I wrote *SimpleBiz360*™. Times, technology, culture, music, arts, housing and clothing change, but human relations principles remain relatively unchanged generation to generation.

Genuine Enthusiasm can make you money. I did a fair amount of public speaking at Northeastern universities in the late 1980's when I was a recruiter and sales trainer. On my third trip back to Ithaca College to speak, a professor set me up and advertised me as an evening of "**Infotainment**." I spoke to about 85 students and some faculty from her Organizational and Behavioral classes.

I spoke on the topics of *business reality, transferrable skills, goal setting* and *enthusiasm*. The professor had each attendee write me a brief recap of what they thought of the evening. When I got this 21-page report, I thought that *transferrable skills* would dominate the feedback. Very few touched on that. Resoundingly, 68% (58) of the students focused on *Enthusiasm* with 100% positive remarks. The topic was fresh and inspiring to them. It was contagious in a very healthy and skill-building way!

Genuine Enthusiasm tends to be overlooked by many businesses, but the **CUSTOMERS** want to see it. They want to get excited about their possible investment. When a business owner displays authentic **Enthusiasm,** it spills out to potential **CUSTOMERS**, and that **Enthusiasm** becomes contagious.

You can learn to become energized about what you do. Trust the Frank Bettger story. **Genuine Enthusiasm** will make you money and lead to **Repeat** and **Referral Customers**.

CUSTOMER TOOLS 63–94

63. Demonstrate respect for the **TIME** of the customer.

64. Demonstrate respect for the **MONEY** of the customer.

65. Give customers your **UNDIVIDED ATTENTION**.

66. Recognize the customer by **NAME**.

67. Take adequate **NOTES** while working with customers.

68. Keep **POLITICS** out of customer interactions.

69. Create **EASY-TO-USE** on-line customer products and services.

70. Find ways to **THANK** customers often.

71. Express customer appreciation with **SINCERITY**.

72. **LEARN** a little about your customer.

73. Demonstrate genuine **INTEREST** in the life of your customer.

74: **RECIPROCATE** when customers show interest in your life.

75. Work on being **LIKEABLE.**

76. **ELIMINATE** conduct that creates customer tension.

77. **DRESS** in industry appropriate apparel.

78. **GROOM** in an industry appropriate manner.

79. Use appropriate **TABLE MANNERS**.

80. Answer the customer question: **What's in it for me (WIIFM)**?

81. Understand the five-step **BUYING PROCESS.**

82. Ask for the business (**DIRECT** or **ALTERNATE**).

83. Don't take a customer **NO** personally.

84. Be prepared for **NO ANSWER** (the new no).

85. Understand how **Evidence DEFEATS Disbelief**.

86. Learn to become **COMFORTABLE** using evidence.

87. Create and use a business **TRAVEL** proof/evidence portfolio.

88. Create and use a business **CYBER** proof/evidence portfolio.

89. Develop an **APPRECIATION PROGRAM** for customers.

90. Devote **FRIDAY AFTERNOONS** to checking on customers.

91. Learn to volunteer an **APOLOGY** when necessary.

92. Resolve conflicts **FACTUALLY**, not emotionally.

93. Build issue resolution on **REALISTIC** capabilities.

94. Choose your words and **SPEAKING TONE** carefully.

PROCEDURES establish sequential order to repetitive business actions. These reduce mistakes, deliver consistency, ensure reliable profitability and create operational stability.

TOOLS 95–137

In the last 15 years, the amount of time I spend solving problems has increased. Today, I work for six different companies and spend a minimum average of two hours per day troubleshooting. Spearheading the corrective efforts is necessary but chews up quality time and effort. The real aggravation is that many of these back-pedaling, fix-it situations could be avoided.

As solopreneurs and small business owners, our success is determined by our ability to move forward swiftly and profitably. Going backwards to clean up situations from old transactions is costly and destructive to our financial health. Real life business encounters reveal time and time again that mistakes are directly correlated to a few simple principles. My conclusions are twofold:

- Number one, when I reverse engineer these issues, I find that often, the dots connect to a lack of clear, pre-established and well documented **Expectations**.

- Number two, in many cases there seems to be a lack of **PROCEDURES**. For many decades, companies referred to these as "standard operating procedures" (SOPs), which is an old term and acronym. In recent decades this concept is also described as a "process performance standard."

Consider this scenario from when I was Executive Vice President with an apparel manufacturer: The fifth hour of my first day on the job, I was confronted with two problems that were bigger than anything I had ever been asked to solve by any company.

Problem #1: A major retailer had returned 96,000 pants because we substituted the approved fabric for a cheaper material. The cheaper 100% Cotton Twill with a wrinkle resistant finish didn't meet the approved fabric specifications. We were fired from this large replenishment pant program (**Repeat Customer**).

Problem #2: We owned 318,000 yards of distressed fabric we bought at a discount to service the replenishment pant program we lost.

The daily dose of problems with this company went on day after day after day for the next two-and-a-half years. I spent inordinate amounts of time correcting old problems and self-induced calamities. Things were so bad at one point, we could not even send our salespeople into the field to meet with customers for 14 or 15 months. When we began to travel, I personally met with store owners to apologize for mishandling their business orders for the past year or so. Almost every customer meeting started with carting me off to a room behind closed doors where these owners shot me with rubber bullets, yelled at me, cursed at me and lambasted our company that entire time. Sad but true!

Why? What causes this much chaos requiring so much time to fix? This company paralyzed itself. Consistently, the arrows would point back to poor **PROCEDURES** or no **PROCEDURES** at all.

Scanning the totality of my career, a stark similarity kept popping up—workers perform the same tasks differently. This creates variations in how repetitive actions or processes are performed. The results can be messy, costly and unpleasant to customers. These operational variations can create two costly possibilities:

1) Open the door (wide) for the **SBK**.
2) Lead to hours of back-pedaling and clean-up.

Here is the rub! We (20 million solopreneurs) don't have the luxury of dealing with a stream of daily problems that, in many cases, can be avoided. We wear many hats, so we need to focus on getting a multitude of things done to satisfy customers and keep them coming back. Trust me, we will have plenty of problems to solve. We need issues to occupy a minimum amount of daily time.

Here is a practical example of a **PROCEDURE**. This is what I have used for many years when processing orders. A step-by-step order entry process like this also helps if your solopreneur enterprise expands and you mushroom into a small business with multiple employees. The new associates are free to showcase their individual personalities without sacrificing the quality of service because they all follow the same process.

Example: Order Entry Procedure

STEP #1 – Email to Customer (before order entry):

a) Confirm purchase order receipt.
b) Assure customer that order will be entered ASAP.
c) Confirm that estimated ship date will be emailed.
d) Confirm that back order (BO) information will be emailed.
e) **Copy Jeff Mason.**

STEP #2 – Email to Customer:

a) After order entry – Advise expected ship date.
b) After order entry – Advise items/quantity of BO.
c) If there are BO's – Advise estimated ship dates.
d) Ask customer if we keep BO's on order or cancel.
e) **Copy Jeff Mason.**

STEP #3 – Email to Customer:

a) Confirm receipt of customer answer to Step #2.

b) **Copy Jeff Mason.**

STEP #4 – Email to Customer (if BO's):

a) Advise customer when the BO's are in-house.

b) Advise customer of expected ship date.

c) **Copy Jeff Mason.**

STEP #5 – OPTIONAL – Writing to Customer:

a) Advise customer when the BO's shipped.

b) Advise customer of BO shipment carrier + tracking #.

c) **Copy Jeff Mason.**

This is a real-life example of how you let a **PROCEDURE** or **PROCESS** dictate a rhythm and protocol for how you handle certain repetitive business processes. This removes personal preference and installs sequential order to the business task. Let's unpack this example from above a little further:

1) Your business receives orders at info@simplebiz360.com.

2) Your business responds from info@simplebiz360.com.

3) Your electronic signature is from you, the owner.

Consider what happens if you get the flu and are out for two days. Someone else does the order entry while you are sick.

If this associate follows these steps, the customer never knows you were sick. **Why?** Orders get processed the same way every day no matter who performs the function.

Imagine if you grow and expand needing to hire a new employee? After assimilation to your order-taking **PROCEDURE**, the result will be successful.

Let the **PROCEDURE** or **PROCESS** do the work for you and your company.

My mission is to help you by introducing simple, repetitious, habitual **PROCEDURES** that maximize customer satisfaction, conserve time and deliver healthy financial results.

Expectations play a significant role is establishing these dependable processes and **PROCEDURES**. **Expectations** and **Procedures** are related. I encourage you to periodically revisit and revise your Expectations to help solidify sound **PROCEDURES**.

Margin Erosion

Lack of **PROCEDURES** directly connects to loss of hard-earned profitability through **Margin Erosion**. This term represents pennies, nickels, dimes and quarters that are used to pay for unplanned mistakes and issues. This money belongs to your gross profit but must be used instead to finance the mistakes. You can't always see this spelled out in front of you as it happens a little here and a little there. These monies add up and can be scary once you quantify them.

I'll give you a great example in my life when I reached out to super nice people at a local small business:

- I called a tree service company for an estimate.
- The owner took my call and came out that day to quote.
- $425 covered tree/branch removal plus stump grinding.
- The owner plus two associates performed service next day.
- They determined a stump grinding machine was needed.
- I paid partial fee of $350.
- Day 12 — The company sent a stump grinder via truck.
- Machine was too wide to fit through fence opening.
- Technician left, not having accomplished stump grinding.
- Stump grinding required a sub-contractor.
- Day 56 — They arrive (after eight text messages + three calls).
- Technician pulled up with a rented stump grinder on a trailer.
- The job was finished in one hour.
- The owner promised to invoice me.
- Day 87 — I had still not received an invoice.

Where is the **Margin Erosion** in this scenario?

- Day 12 — time to prepare, load, deploy and return truck.
- Day 12 — gas used in truck for roundtrip #1.
- Day 12 — loss of billable technician time on another paying job.
- Day 56 — loss of billable technician time on another paying job.
- Day 56 — time to prepare, load, deploy and return truck.
- Day 56 — gas used in truck for roundtrip #2.

By the 87th day, I was never billed for the final $75.00. I voluntarily sent a $75.00 check to the company owner the following day.

The point of this 88-day story is to illuminate that a tremendous amount of money was lost because the owner did not incorporate one, simple **PROCEDURE** when he quoted my job. This illustration has nothing to do with people, it has everything to do with sound **PROCEDURES** making you money and satisfying customers. The owner and his son are men of good character, but their company is losing money.

What is the **Margin Erosion** value of this situation? I don't know the cost structure, but I can safely say that the owner relinquished $75.00 of profitability to rent this huge stump grinder. In addition to the $75.00 loss, I'd say the owner has another 5%–15% of margin loss. Multiply this type of costly event (lack of **PROCEDURE**) twice per week for 50 weeks, and there is quite a bit of lost money.

What **PROCEDURE** can help this tree service to prevent this exact **Margin Erosion** in the future? In my opinion it is simple: Measure every fence opening on each potential job the company quotes.

This kind of scenario is the very reason I am so excited to write *SimpleBiz360*™. I want to help you avoid these painful outcomes. By implementing a few simple **Improvement** concepts, your company can be more profitable and give you a better return on time and money spent.

Handful of Sand

When and if you visit the beach, try this simple exercise: Grab a handful of dry sand (the finer the sand, the better), tightly clench your hand and bring your closed fist up to your eye level. For the next few seconds, watch the tiny crystals fall out of your grasp and land on the ground. Those scattered particles represent coins (pennies, nickels, dimes and quarters) that quietly disappear from your business. This lost money diminishes the financial success of your business. Hold on to your sand!

Details

I had the pleasure of working for Atlanta-based Oxford Industries from 1992–2000. This terrific company taught me many best practice principles. It took me eight interviews to get my job. I am serious! Two of my eight interviews were focused on "**Details**." I could not understand why **Details** garnered this much questioning. Once hired by Oxford, I soon learned that as a publicly-owned company, they were responsible to the shareholders to meet their bottom-line earnings projections as close as possible. **To do so, Detail Management was essential.** Take a look at these high-level objectives Oxford used to meet the desired end goal:

a) Be detail-oriented in everything.
b) Prevent manufacturing mistakes.
c) Prevent customer chargebacks due to mistakes.
d) Limit margin erosion and operational cost variances.
e) Deliver what customers paid for and satisfy shareholders.

How did we do this? **PROCEDURES**! That's right...we put standard **PROCEDURES** into place. Our mission to please retail partners and company stockholders steered us to focus on **Details** and bring sequential order to repetitive processes. We avoided the dreaded margin erosion. We controlled our variances and prevented potential calamities to the best of our proactive abilities.

You want this! **PROCEDURES** will be your trusted allies. You don't want margin erosion and the avalanche of issues that come sliding down the hill with it.

Lastly, **PROCEDURES** help when you expand and hire additional employees. Sound **PROCEDURES** ensure that regardless of who is handling certain operational duties, these functions are performed the same. This is what bakes consistency into your business formula, keeps the **SBKs** away and creates happy customers.

This logo appears on the back of my business cards and on my websites. It defines the way I conduct business. It silently sends a message to customers that I care about their investments and that I will handle their business with diligence.

Why did Oxford Industries conduct two of my eight interviews on **Details**? Because it is part of their business culture and considered essential to their annual success.

After serving this large retail customer for four years, I announced my departure in an email as I had accepted an executive position with another company in St. Louis. This 11/3/2000 email is the actual one this large retailer sent me:

> "Why do the good people always have to leave? You've been wonderful to work with. I was just telling Heather this morning that you and Darrell are my favorites. *If all my vendors had your level of attentiveness and attention to detail, my job would be so much easier!* Thanks for all your hard work and partnership, and good luck in St. Louis. Given that it's such a small world, our paths will most likely cross again."

In a similar situation, I again announced my departure from a company. This 11/23/2005 quote is another that I hold near and dear as confirmation that I am doing right by my customers:

> "We will all miss you. It has been a pleasure working with you. *I wish all our vendors had your efficiency and follow-through.* Best of luck in your new position and have a happy holiday season."

I hold both quotes in the highest regard to this very day. Although the 2000 quote is from a $10,000,000 customer, and the 2005 quote is from a $60,000 client, they carry equal value. **Why?**

1) They validate my passion to be a professional.
2) They reward me for my **Detail Management.**
3) They show my commitment regardless of account stature.
4) They prove **Attention to Detail** matters to customers.

Detail Management will earn, yes *earn* you, long-term **Repeat** and **Referral Customers. Why?** Because customers respond favorably to businesses that protect their investments and make their jobs easier. Good follow-through **Tools** are also close relatives to **PROCEDURES.**

Paying attention to **Details** will keep you away from **SBKs** and the cliff where your revenues disappear into the ravine of *Lost Customers*.

3x5 Syndrome

The appetite for managing details seems to be giving way to speed and instant access. This evaporating interest in details is a rising **SBK** that is slowly creeping into every nook and cranny of our business world. From smartphone technology to convenience lines, remote controls, simultaneous newsfeeds and streaming social media, we have become slaves to quick and easy, and we run from tedium. If we cannot read something that fits in our 3" x 5" phone windows, and we cannot read it in 12 seconds...we lose interest! I have labeled this mobile device management the **3x5 Syndrome.**

Through diligent observation and plenty of experience, I assure you this needs to be addressed in your business. By running your daily company affairs on a smartphone, you are risking an increase in mistakes and necessary, back-peddling clean-up. I have tackled many issues caused by the **3x5 Syndrome.** Additionally, I have also been sucked into using the phone instead of my laptop resulting in dozens of minor snafus.

Why is the **3x5 Syndrome** something to recognize and avoid? Because it opposes attention-to-detail. Attachments, line item reporting, clarity, font size, email thread chronology, Inbox filing and overall content can be easily mismanaged resulting in expensive future corrections. There are plenty of professionals who will argue my point. Guaranteed exceptions to my claim exist far and wide.

Don't get me wrong, I use my phone every single day for business. However, I use it for simple tasks like email receipt confirmations or identifying issues that need immediate attention. If a customer is in a jam I want to know about it, so I see it on the phone and I start the resolution effort immediately. However, if it requires reading and interpreting critical, highly detailed information embedded in reports, I save it until I log on to my laptop. Plenty of clients receive my smartphone email responses that look like this: "Thank you for your email. I will give you a quality and detailed response when I arrive at my hotel tonight. Thank you for your patience and understanding."

Do you really want to roll the dice and run your company in that 3"x 5" mobile device universe?

Compounding this **3x5 Syndrome** is the apparent increase in business professionals being inaccessible and being absent without their laptops or tablets. The icing on the cake is the rise of automated emails like the following:

> "I will be away from the office for an extended period of time and have limited access to my email. I will answer your emails upon my return."

I'm sorry, but in this day and age, this type of **SWIICFU** (Service When It Is Convenient For Us) messaging is a kiss of death for a solopreneur or small business owner. The **SBK** will be knocking on the door in rapid fashion with this cavalier approach. Our culture is being conditioned to pursue the quick and easy at home and in our private lives. The danger is to let this cultural shift blend in with your professional life. Fewer professionals are committed to getting into the weeds than ten years ago. It's only going to get worse. Please don't jump on this bandwagon!

Personally, I travel with my laptop and diligently respond to every email, every day. If I pull into my hotel after a long drive at 11:00 p.m., I crank up my laptop and stay online until 12:30 a.m. or wake up at 5:30 a.m. to answer electronic correspondence.

Why? Because I believe it is my duty to the good people who trust me with their investments. I MUST do this. How could I shun them and blow them off? I feel the same way if a person from one of my six companies asks me about something. They are entitled to a rapid and quality response. I am their investment, and I owe them the same respect I give a paying client.

Customers don't often share feedback on small appreciations, but in the quiet of their office on any given work day, many appreciate professionals who manage business promptly, effectively and with a respect for customer time. Believe it or not, this business approach will actually seem fresh to consumers because they don't experience it very often! You will stand out and shine brighter than eight of your ten competitors. Take diligent care of time and money investments that buyers devote to your goods or services. Demonstrate respect for customers by reducing and eliminating the need to chase you down for information.

Here is some good news! If you agree to get into the weeds and become a **Doctor of Details**, chances are very high that your **Repeat Customer** base will flourish and your **Referral Customer** base will be bountiful. As solopreneurs and small business owners, we don't have the luxury of saying we are inaccessible for an undefined length of time without the ability to be reached. We have to embrace crossing those T's and dotting those I's each and every day.

Embrace **Detail Management** by creating simple **PROCEDURES** safeguarding against using your mobile devices in critical instances rather than your computer, laptop or tablet. Also consider baking these **PROCEDURES** into your **Core Values** or **Expectations** that you share with customers.

PROCEDURE TOOLS 95–137

Create the following:

95. **ORDER ENTRY** instructions (step-by-step).
96. Product warehouse **PACKING** instructions (step-by-step).
97. Product **RETURN** instructions (step-by-step).
98. **ISSUE RESOLUTION** format.
99. Descriptive **WARRANTY** policy.
100. **QUOTE** template for quick, consistent use.
101. Content **PROTOCOLS** for issuing written quotes.

102. In-house **AUDIT** protocols to ensure consistency.

103. **QUALITY CONTROL** protocols ensure consistent quality.

104. User-friendly and effective **CREDIT APPLICATIONS**.

105. **ONE-TOUCH** management protocols.

106. **ELECTRONIC** file cabinets for each customer.

107. Informative and polite **VOICEMAIL** message.

108. **SELL SHEETS** for all primary products.

109. Flyer **TEMPLATES** for consistency and rapid design.

110. **NEW PRODUCT** flyers for invoices and product shipments.

111. Consistent **INVOICE RELEASE** protocols.

112. **PUNCTUAL** invoice distribution protocols.

113. Customer-friendly product **TERMINOLOGY**.

114. **ITEM #s** for all products and services.

115. Marry **EXPECTATIONS** and **PROCEDURES**.

116. Consider **NOTE JOURNALS** for long-term record keeping.

117. Set up **EMAIL TEMPLATES** for future time conservation.

118. Embed **BRAND MESSAGING** wherever appropriate.

119. Include **COUNTRY OF ORIGIN** on all packaging.

120. Commit to **ANSWER** 100% of inbox emails consistently.

121. **SORT** and **FILE** emails on a regular basis.

122. **USE** consistent product terminology.

123. **DISPLAY** item #'s on all print and digital platforms.

Wholesaler Procedure Tools:

124. Create hi-resolution **DIGITAL ASSETS** for all products.

125. Set up a **DIGITAL ASSET MANAGEMENT (DAM)** site.

126. Establish consistent layout **FORMAT** for digital assets.

127. **ASSIGN** edition #s to each print or digital catalog.

128. Invest in **PURCHASING** authentic UPC codes.

129. Obtain authentic **G1 CERTIFICATES** for UPC codes.

130. Apply **DUAL** UPC label for retail + ecommerce.

131. Ensure UPC codes are also **HUMAN READABLE (HR)**.

132. Affix HR + Barcode UPCs on **INNER** product packaging.

133. Place HR + Barcode UPCs on **OUTER** product packaging.

134. **PRE-TEST** UPC barcode labeling to ensure reliable scanning.

135. Apply **PROP 65** labeling on all applicable products.

136. Use hi-resolution **IMAGERY** for each color (no color chips).

137. Develop user-friendly **ON-LINE** ordering processes.

Follow-up and follow-through are essential
for successful customer SERVICE delivery.

TOOLS 133–163

SBK = Silent Business Killer

Always Servicing

If you want to maintain and grow your small business, then please accept that providing **SERVICE** is a constant function. Providing **SERVICE** never sleeps! It never stops. You never stop. Providing timely and professional **SERVICE** will separate you from competitors. In fact, good **Service Providers** will look and feel like something fresh or new. **Why?** Go back to the **SBK** model. The answer is because customers don't feel like they will get good **SERVICE**, and they have been feeling that way for decades.

To highlight good customer care, I feel compelled to illustrate the *bad*.

SWIICFU
(Service When It Is Convenient For Us)

This is a major element in the modern work world.

Some companies don't care that **Customer Service** requests go unanswered. It is a dangerous trend that is large and in charge in 2019 commerce. In my opinion, it has been growing and mushrooming for the past few decades. That is why you see it front and center in the **SBK** model. Generally speaking, consumers have been conditioned to expect no satisfaction if they complain about inadequate **SERVICE**.

Don't leave it up to a customer to pester you for **SERVICE**. After decades of receiving poor assistance and care from corporations, many customers just avoid company contact altogether. So often the customer muddles through their unpleasant transaction and never comes back. Consider these four snapshots:

---

1. I worked for a company that did this:

- Customer service erased unread emails before going home.
- They forced customer to email or call again.
- This pattern could repeat itself for days and days.

Think I'm kidding? Absolutely not!

---

2. I worked for a company that did this:

- Management chose which service questions to answer.
- The company told me, "The squeaky wheel gets the oil."
- I'd call and email multiple times spanning days and weeks.
- Eventually my persistence would produce feedback.

Think I'm kidding? Absolutely not!

---

3. I worked for a company that did this:

- A customer shipping charge question took 46 days to answer.
- The solution required 42 emails and six phone calls.
- On day 46, I called company owner for overdue feedback.
- Besides myself, no one ever apologized to the customer.

Think I'm kidding? Absolutely not!

---

4. I worked for a company that did this:

• 4200 units were delivered requiring 36 warranty repairs.
• Our dealer resolved six warranty claims in first 120 days.
• The manufacturer took over warranty service on day 121.
• Zero claims were resolved between days 121 and 180.
• The customer reached a boiling point on day 180.
• I took control of managing all remaining claims (30).
• In the next 60 days, all claims were completed.

Think I'm kidding? Absolutely not!

I could go on and on! Literally…I have hundreds and hundreds of "Don't service this way" stories. I will bolster **Customer Service Tools** with more references and stories in this chapter and in upcoming podcasts.

There are huge opportunities to win lots of **Repeat** and **Referral Customers** with quality and professional **SERVICE**. Boiling down to the framework for customer-satisfying **SERVICE**, these are the **"must do"** and **_"must avoid"_** building blocks for delivering **GREAT SERVICE**.

Must <u>DO</u> Service Building Blocks

1) Get to customers **BEFORE** they get to you.
2) Tell customers what they **DESERVE** to hear.
3) Deliver prompt **FOLLOW-UP**.
4) Deliver competent **FOLLOW-THROUGH**.
5) Use **PROFESSIONAL** words and attitude.
6) Tune into radio station **WIIFM**, "What's In It For Me?"

Must <u>AVOID</u> at All Costs

A. *Make the customer pester you for feedback.*

B. *Tell the customer what you think they want to hear.*

C. *Take your time in delivering customer follow-up.*

D. *Provide choppy, cryptic and confusing information.*

E. *Respond in a condescending, rude, pompous or sarcastic tone.*

F. *Focus on what you want instead of what satisfies the customer.*

I don't want to say providing good **SERVICE** is easy. However, it is definitely not hard. All it needs is your commitment.

We have all heard the cliché over and over: **"Treat people how you would want to be treated."** This idea is absolutely applicable to business today. Rewind back to the **Expectations** chapter. When you are at your quiet thinking place (beach, park, or favorite chair), bend your mind and contemplate…really think hard… how do you want to be treated? Don't forget: This is your business! You financed your company with inheritance money, took out a second mortgage, used years of savings…whatever the case. Do you really want to subject your investment of time and money to being noted for giving crappy **SERVICE**?

Or…do you want to secure long-term **Repeat** and great **Referral Customers**? You know the answer! So again, use the skills you have, implement **Tools** in this book and weave them into your thinking when you are in reflective thought about your business.

#1: Get to Buyers Before They Get to You

It has been my experience, in most cases, when I contact the customer first, potential issues seem to be diffused almost immediately. **Why?** I believe it is because they sense I genuinely care about their transaction, money and time.

Phone Call Example

CUSTOMER: Hello!

BUSINESS SERVICE CALLER: Hello Mrs. Jones, this is Mike Morgan from the Morgan Blind Company. I hope all is well. Do you have a quick minute, or is this a bad time?

CUSTOMER: No, I have a minute.

BUSINESS SERVICE CALLER: Great. The purpose of my call is to let you know that the blind manufacturer called me today and informed me that the delivery to my warehouse is going to be a week late. Apparently, the factory is still waiting for some custom metal clips that have not arrived to them. We really apologize for this delay! So, with that being said, I am looking to do the install on the 21st as opposed to the 14th. Actually, to be safe, could you give me two extra days in case the manufacturer is off by a day or two? Maybe we do the install on the 23rd? Will that work for you?

CUSTOMER: Let me check my calendar…Yes, the 23rd will work just fine. What time?

BUSINESS SERVICE CALLER: Terrific! Let's plan on 10:00 AM. Will this work?

CUSTOMER: 10:00 AM will be perfect!

BUSINESS SERVICE CALLER: Great. It is the 5th of the month today, so please expect a call from me on the 12th. The purpose of that call will be to give you an update on the blinds to make sure everything is still on schedule for installing on the 23rd.

CUSTOMER: Okay. Well, thank you for calling me to let me know all of this. I really appreciate it!

BUSINESS SERVICE CALLER: It is my pleasure, Mrs. Jones. Again, we are so sorry about the delay. Have a great day, and have a nice weekend.

CUSTOMER: You also. Thanks again for the call!

***

After the hang up, I can hear the following exchange as though the dialogue is taking place in my own home:

UPSTAIRS: Who was that sweetie?

DOWNSTAIRS: It was Mike Morgan from the blind company.

UPSTAIRS: Is everything alright?

DOWNSTAIRS: Oh yeah…Mike was just calling to let me know the blinds are not going to be here in time to do the installation on the 14th, so we moved the install to the 23rd.

UPSTAIRS: Oh. Okay. Did you call them, or did they call you?

DOWNSTAIRS: The owner, Mike, called me.

UPSTAIRS: Well, that was nice of him to give you a heads-up.

DOWNSTAIRS: Agreed…They are the nicest people over there!

This is what **"Get to customers before they get to you"** is all about.

Assuming Mike follows through with the call on the 12th, and the installation goes well on the 23rd, this is a ripe example of where **Referral** business will come knocking eventually. Certainly, this could generate nice pictures and a reference letter. However, and most importantly, there will be no **SBK** in this scenario. None…nada…not possible! Mr. and Mrs. Jones were respected. Their hard-earned money was respected. Their time was respected, and they never had to pester Mike for **SERVICE**!

BINGO! I assure you, once this stuff works for your business, a **SERVICE** contagiousness will evolve. Satisfying customers will become fun, rewarding and generate well deserved **Repeat** and **Referral** business.

#2: Tell Buyers What They Deserve to Hear

You are managing customer money with each transaction. They are giving their hard-earned income to you in exchange for something you sell. Respect that process! Respect that money! Respect that client! If you want to grow and stay in business, tell people purchasing your products what they deserve to hear. Start right now! You will be amazed with the results.

My career is full of instances where I told customers what they deserved to hear. Buyers applauded me many times for being honest, upfront and realistic with them. Yet, more often than not, the clients never said a word to me or thanked me. However, I am convinced that at night when their heads hit the pillows, they felt comfortable giving me their money in exchange for the goods and **SERVICE** I provided.

Good news is easy and pleasing to release. Bad news is difficult to convey, but buyers and decision makers need to hear it so they can manage their affairs effectively. If your business conduct follows this simple rule, you will gain a reputation as an honest operator, and you will get new business because people will speak favorably of you. **This is the reverse** of the **SBK** model.

These four situations from my career prove the importance of being transparent with customers:

Example #1

In 1996, our company legal department called me to advise that we had overcharged one of my customers about $72 for a Canadian GST tax issue. The customer was small and ordered infrequently. My associate from the legal department even chuckled at the insignificant amount. Nonetheless, we both agreed to send the $72 to the customer as it was their money.

ACTION: The check was sent to the customer (buyer) who was blown away that I would take the time to send such a small check.

REWARD: This $72 went on to create a robust annual sales volume. The buyer liked the honesty and trustworthiness and awarded me with much more business. In the years to follow, I continued to **SERVICE** this customer through a new buyer and soon did over $2,000,000 a year with this customer. That new buyer became a friend, an associate, and is responsible for the photos you see on the front and back cover of this book!

Example #2

In 1997, I discovered that I would be a few days late on a private label order for a new customer. Our production time took about 180 days, and I discovered this issue in the third week of production.

ACTION: I advised the buyer of this condition, and she was amazed that I asked for an extension five months before delivery. The buyer liked the honesty as it gave her time to shift her store ads for the week of the adjusted delivery. This was easy to do because she had notice well in advance. The buyer even told me stories about account executives that would never tell her they were late. As a result, she would get a black eye with management, and her store ads would be all messed up and filled with rainchecks.

REWARD: The buyer was impressed by my honesty and started to shop me regularly and give me seasonal orders. At one point, and based on her trust in me, I was invited to fly to their HQ to give a business seminar to all the apparel buyers across all categories.

Example #3

In 2014, I started representing a company that took notoriously long (30 days) to ship orders. The industry norm for these types of "at once" retail products is one to seven days.

ACTION: I advised every potential new customer of our 30-day delivery cycle. Almost every buyer seemed surprised at the timeline. However, if they signed up, they did so with the knowledge of the realistic order fulfillment.

REWARD: Buyers from various industries began to sign on with my new line. All orders were written to deliver in 30 days. My sales grew to almost $900,000 in my second year with almost zero delivery complaints or grumblings.

Example #4

In 2010, I started working for a company that would ask sales representatives to promote new products and secure early orders far in advance of our expected shipment dates. The company would establish aggressive fulfillment timelines and ask us to use these with our customers. During a discussion with one of the senior reps (Rich), he suggested that I would do myself and my customers a favor if I was to add 12 months to every delivery date issued by the company.

Rich was with the company for 17 years and witnessed consistent company failures in achieving initial product launch dates. He managed his accounts by adding 365 days to every launch date estimate and created happy customers in the process.

I initially trusted the company and asked all my customers to give me orders based on the production calendar I was given. In 2011, I looked back, and sure enough, Rich was correct. Every delivery of new styles took approximately 12 months longer than the company instructed me.

ACTION: In 2011, I began to add one year to every new product delivery date issued by the company.

REWARD: My customers were never angry with me for overpromising and under-delivering. Because I added a full calendar year (Thank you Rich!), the new products appeared almost to the month I said they would. My territory was complaint-free. I watched and listened to other reps who were constantly chit-chatting about griping by dealers due to very tardy new product deliveries.

Their appreciation for realistic **SERVICE** will always outweigh telling buyers what they want to hear and delivering something entirely different.

#3: Deliver Prompt Follow-Up

Customers want to know you understand them. They want to know you hear them. They want to know you got their voicemail or email. They want to know you are making sure their investment is not going to be wasted. They want to know you care.

What is the reward if you answer all the above calls for duty? Most likely, a healthy, thriving and growth-oriented business.

From 2000–2003, I was Executive Vice President of a medium-sized company in the law enforcement products business. Although I was responsible for sales, marketing, product development, and **Customer Service**, my primary focus was sales. During my three years in this capacity, 50% of my sales positions were held by factory employees. The other 50% was with independent (commission only) representatives. I had some good independent reps and some marginal ones. This 50/50 representative mix was indicative of the industry.

What I came to realize is that almost every complaint about poor representation was targeted at independent representatives. The complaints were consistently centered on *POOR FOLLOW-UP*. My managerial observations confirmed this. My takeaway was that I could make a good living if I could represent various manufacturing companies as an independent sales representative. My confidence was strong as I focused on raising the bar of my follow-up **SERVICE** skills in previous years. With that enhanced skill set foundation, and professional follow-up as my centerpiece, the decision to open my own sales agency was cemented as a firm plan of action.

My instincts were right. In 2008, I started the North59 Sales Agency that has been lucrative and productive since I opened my doors. **Why?** I truly believe my primary success factor is due to my consistency in following up in a timely manner. I felt and behaved differently than 80-90% of my competition. My dealers (resellers) rewarded me for that attitude to timely follow-up.

❖ KEY FOLLOW-UP TIP

Treat every email, voice message or text like a face-to-face conversation. If you were standing next to someone and they asked you a question, you would answer it as you stand in the presence of that person. If you didn't, it would be awkward.

Imagine if someone standing next to you expressed a business concern, and you just stared blankly into space or at their face without a response. That would be a weird situation. Learn to process client emails, voice messages and text messages like you are communicating in the same room together. Handle these follow-ups promptly, directly and comprehensively.

You will take your business to the next level when you follow up without being asked. Remember, get to the customer before they get to you. That is when customers really begin to recognize your reputation and pass it on to other friends and relatives. Becoming a champion at following up will earn you a positive perception in the marketplace and ensure your reputation as a *Professional*. The **SBK** will wreak very little havoc on your business if you master prompt follow-up.

#4: Deliver Competent Follow-Through

Following up takes commitment. Following through takes rolling up your sleeves and delivering tangible results, good or bad. Competency is relevant as you must attempt to address the customer needs head-on. You must cover all your bases, review all the variables, consider different solutions and present your customer with the most comprehensive feedback to assist in their informed decision.

Once you are able to combine follow-up and follow-through, customers really take notice.

The first time this became evident to me was with my Kohl's buyer. I had worked for five years to obtain business from Kohl's. Finally, I earned various private label programs and began a three-year stint doing millions in annual business. I vividly recall a landmark event in my career with Kohl's. My buyer and I scheduled a day and time to review a multitude of points that needed decisions or updates. However, my buyer could only give me ten minutes of his time. He asked me to send him the topics in advance via fax.

I wrote a seven-point document with all the variables presented. I faxed it to him prior to our meeting and then called him. When he answered the phone, he literally shouted out his approval and said, "This is perfect! This is exactly how I wanted you to present it."

My Kohl's buyer was a classic "doer." About nine minutes later, we were done. He was so happy with me, and I was equally pleased because I had detailed answers to all seven areas of questioning.

More importantly for my career, I had a recipe for conducting follow-through for the rest of my years in business. I still follow that recipe to this day because of the resounding and impressionable approval I received from my Kohl's buyer.

Results are the crowning achievement of follow-through. End results won't always be good. That is okay…you cannot always achieve the exact outcome a customer wants to hear and experience. However, you can always follow through to produce results.

❖ KEY FOLLOW-THROUGH TIP

Conduct follow-through in writing. To the best of your ability, avoid delivering follow-through via text messaging. **Why?** Number one, text message trails are often deleted. Number two, certain follow-up requires detail that is hard to embed in text messages. Number three, there are extra steps to follow if you are going to take screen shots of text messages and save them and send them to buyers as email attachments. Based on knowing the current speed and pace of business, screen shot management will be hard to execute as a standard process.

Solopreneurs and small business owners need to touch something once to keep pace with the speedy rhythm of modern-day business. My hunch is that at some point text message follow-through could result in a costly margin erosion event. I am sure there are many skilled people capable of managing text messaging follow-through competently. I am definitely not one of those solopreneurs. All I ask is that you consider these three cautionary points before setting up your follow-through procedures.

After providing follow-through on the phone, write the customer a bullet-style recap of the conversation. SAVE...SAVE...SAVE this follow-through correspondence. In fact, this is exactly how I followed up with my Kohl's buyer in the previous example. I recommend emails. I cannot tell you how many times saving follow-through correspondence has assisted me. On many occasions I have been asked by clients to resend recaps and follow-through decisions months later. In fact, this helped me with a huge situation with a major retailer. You will hear more about this in a podcast.

You will stand out among your business peers as an exceptional **Service Provider** when you consistently deliver results, solutions, updates and decisions with professional follow-through.

#5: Use Professional Words and Attitude

Be careful how you speak and write to customers. Learn how to use professional words, terms and phrases. Most of all, be respectful and polish what you say with a business-like attitude.

Avoid slang and industry terms that only you and your vendor base understand. Always put yourself on the receiving end of what you are going to write or say.

We currently are in the throngs of people and businesses who make horrible word choices. Many of the words are casual and end up causing major damage control after they are written or spoken. We are in a day and age where your words can go viral; they never disappear, and they will haunt you until your last day on earth. Carefully choose what you put on social media. You cannot take it back.

Protect your business and your reputation with appropriate and professional word selection. Learn to exchange lazy and weak for appropriate and effective words. I am not suggesting to be tricky, but try a couple of these word substitutions in your next efforts:

- Exchange the word *problem* with the word **issue**.
- Exchange the word *buy* with the word **invest**.
- Exchange the word *bad* with the word **unsatisfactory**.

These are just a few examples. Review some of your standard correspondence and challenge yourself to identify weak words. Then, look for alternatives that are a better fit. My guess is you will find a few opportunities for improvement that jump off the pages.

The attitude you display when **SERVICING** is also very important. How we say things often carries more weight than what we say. Go back and review your **Core Values** and ensure that many are embedded in your written and verbal communication. Politeness, kindness, respectfulness and other bedrock values should be on full display during your interactions.

There is a huge difference in how customers perceive attitude in writing compared to our verbal communication. Customers can't hear text messages, emails and flyers. This is to our disadvantage as business owners. Customers are left to draw their own conclusions about our attitudes. Often times, we come off the opposite of our intentions.

Back in the late 1990's I communicated daily with a customer service team in our Hong Kong office. We had just transitioned from faxing all communication to emailing. Emails were a new way of doing business for our company, so we had to learn and stumble through. Personally, I found it too time consuming to shift from uppercase to lowercase on my keyboard. So, I just typed everything to my Hong Kong office in ALL CAPS.

When I finally travelled to Hong Kong and met my production team, I was confronted with a strange reality. At a group lunch, my international associates told me that I was much different in person than their perception throughout our years of corresponding with email. I asked what they meant. Their answer: "You are so much nicer in person because you never yell at us." Huh?

Well, it turns out my ALL CAPS writing style was perceived as yelling. Imagine, every day and night for a long time, these poor people thought I was yelling at them! I felt horrible...literally horrible! My actual attitude was nothing like what came across in my writing. I was truly writing each email with a healthy, pleasant and respectful attitude, yet my decision to use ALL CAPS sent a different message to the readers. Remember to always use professional words, display a good attitude, and consider how it will be perceived once it is opened and unwrapped by the recipient.

Customers are a precious commodity and very costly to replace. They deserve the best attitude you can give them. **Perception IS Reality**, and your business deserves all the positive perception it can get.

#6: Tune into WIIFM

"What's In It For Me?" (**WIIFM**) is how customers see business relationships. Customers give their money to companies after they have weighed the benefits of choosing one enterprise versus another. With thoughtful deliberations, clients are searching for answers that satisfy questions of how their buying decision affects them. Through their prism, they want to know what's in it for them.

Working off the premise that **WIIFM** is the main customer radio station, you need to deliver **SERVICE** that quenches that thirst for client benefits. Any other style of **SERVICE** will drive buyers away and open the door for **SBKs**. Here is a good example.

One of the companies I represent asked a retired employee from operations to help out with a project. The temporary mission required calling and emailing buyers to ask for orders. I was not copied on these electronic efforts. Eventually, one of my potential dealers shared a copy of the email they received. The crux of the correspondence read *"I need one more big deal before I retire."* Sadly, this effort violates all the principles of good **SERVICE** on so many fronts.

First, the words "I" and "me" are self-centered and are direct opposite choices of what need to be used to tune into **WIIFM**. The main sentence in this email used the word "I" multiple times. Secondly, customers, and especially potential customers, are not going to warm up to this at all. **Why?** Because it doesn't satisfy that quest to provide something for the customer. Potential customers don't care two hoots that this guy is nearing retirement. Current customers might, but most will not hand over an order to satisfy his longing to score one last deal before he hands in his front door key. Third, he lied. He was not going to retire; he was well into his post-career lifestyle. I wonder how many recipients of this "Give me orders!" campaign were troubled by these emails. I know at least one who raised an eyebrow.

Be careful not to alienate customers and telegraph selfish motives over customer-focused **SERVICE**. This type of communication campaign also makes the vendor look extremely desperate. Unless you are running a going-out-of-business sale, you want to avoid projecting that your company may be gasping for air. That is a turn-off for sure.

I am convinced that these six suggestions can lay a sturdy foundation for how you execute customer-pleasing **SERVICE**. It's really not that hard, yet so few companies or business professionals operate this way.

Sincere Apologies

You will make mistakes. You will be faced with a crossroad upon making a mistake. Do you accept fault, or do you shift the blame over to someone else? In addition, you will have the opportunity to call the mistake out or avoid the issue altogether.

In my 75,000+ hours of situational business experience, I can tell you without a doubt, this is where **SBKs** eat our lunch and have a field day.

Scenario A (Avoid Ownership):

If you avoid calling out a mistake that has cost a customer time or money, chances are they will not initiate dialogue with you. They will simply go away in what appears to be a quiet fashion. But remember what happens next! When communicating with friends and family, on the phone, via text message or on social media, they will state their displeasure. Your name will become Mud, and you won't even know it is happening. This is a classic **SBK**.

Scenario B (Blame-Shifting):

Instead of owning a mistake, you decide to claim that a supplier is the root cause of the issue (blame-shifting). This happens so often in business. Trust me...I have caught it dozens of time in dialogue and email threads. The funny thing is, more often than not, the customer reads right through the mistruth and knows that you are flat out lying. If you deliver a face-to-face inaccurate accusation, most consumers read your body language. You may think you're getting away with it, but all too often the neon light hanging over your head displaying *"liar"* tells a different story. You are telegraphing the blatant mistruth, and you don't even know it.

Scenario B is extremely entertaining when the blame-shifter tries to pull a fast one on an experienced mother or law enforcement officer. Trust me: This type of behavior will kill your reputation and hurt your company.

I personally saw this chip away at a corporation I worked for. The owner frequently pointed fingers at everyone else when issues arose. He had the audacity to utter this dandy to one of my customers: "We source the world, and everyone across the globe is having these issues." Shortly after this gem, my customer called me in disbelief. "Did you hear him…'the world.' Does he think I believe this? What a bunch of crap!"

What do you think was the major problem with this company? You guessed it…No **Repeat Customers**. We had so many "one & done" customers because everyone knew our ownership shifted fault. Customers rarely came back for seconds.

Transferring the root cause of errors away from the real culprit is another classic example of the **SBK**. If you caused the issue, then own it.

Scenario C (Confess):

Did you ever try admitting you were wrong to a customer? In 1985, I read these words from Dale Carnegie in *How To Win Friends & Influence People*: **"If you are wrong, admit it quickly and emphatically"** (1936). These words jumped off the page! I started using this guiding principle whenever I was faced with a problem or mistake of my own doing.

I bet in my career that I have written over 50 emails with the subject header "MASON APOLOGY." I even write these "MASON APOLOGY" emails if I spell the name of a person incorrectly.

I have not been able to measure the effect apologies have on my business. It is simply too hard to quantify. What I can tell you is that a genuine admittance to owning fault invites **Repeat Customers** and keeps the business ball rolling. **Why?** Because apologies are rare. Apologies are refreshing. Apologizing for mistakes is the right thing to do when you are committed to delivering **SERVICE** the customer deserves.

We have all heard and witnessed people in the news trying to blame everyone else for what is wrong. My wife and I even watched a television program where a car thief was locked inside the vehicle he was trying to steal. Inside the automobile was a camera recording his every move and word. As the police came up to arrest him, the thief squirmed and writhed in the locked vehicle shouting over and over, "I didn't do it. It's not me! I didn't do it."

Buyers, customers and potential customers have watched similar video footage. They have heard all the same societal spinning and have endured their own children tell winding tales of woe. No one seems to want to accept fault. Everyone wants credit for success. Largely absent from our wordsmith manipulations are humility and apologizing.

In my opinion, and for all those reasons stated above, in 2019 when someone hears a sincere apology it sounds and feels new. We are not accustomed to hearing people accept fault and apologize.

Here is a recent email trail that took place in my business:

From: Mason, Jeff
Sent: Friday, May 24, 2019 8:33 AM
To: Katie
Subject: MASON APOLOGY - 5/24/19

Katie,

Hello. Thank for calling me back yesterday. I made the mistake of addressing you as "Miss Katie." I apologize as it is a habit with me as that is what we call my niece in Texas. I'm so sorry.

Jeff

From: Katie
Sent: Friday, May 24, 2019 9:46 AM
To: Mason, Jeff
Subject: RE: MASON APOLOGY - 5/24/19

Hi Jeff,

I didn't even notice yesterday but I truly do appreciate that! I've certainly been addressed in a less than professional manner at times by others so I really appreciate your attention to that—no offense was taken from you though! I know you're conscientious of professionalism so I wouldn't ever assume you're actively trying to be disrespectful.

Katie

❖ KEY APOLOGY TIP

When you are **SERVICING** customers, and you need to call out a mistake you made, do it like Dale Carnegie. Let's say you failed to enter an order five days ago. When you call the customer, it should sound something like this:

CUSTOMER: Hello.

BUSINESS SERVICE CALLER: Hello Mrs. Jones. This is Mike Morgan from the Morgan Blind Company. I hope all is well. Do you have a quick minute for an update on your recent order?

CUSTOMER: Sure, I have a minute.

BUSINESS SERVICE CALLER: Thank you. The purpose of my call is to let you know that I made a huge mistake with your recent order. The bottom line is that I mismanaged my email inbox, and the order you sent on the 15th did not get noticed and entered until the 20th. This is 100% my fault. I'm really sorry!

The result is that I cannot ship your kitchen blind by the 21st as you requested. The best I can do is to ship it overnight on the 23rd so you receive it the 24th. Will this work?

CUSTOMER: No, it won't. I am having a small family gathering on the 22nd, and I needed it by the 21st. I appreciate the call, but I will have to buy an off-the-shelf blind that is a close match to the rest of the blinds. Please cancel the order.

BUSINESS SERVICE CALLER: Again, I am so sorry. I feel terrible, and I wish I could change the outcome of my mistake. I am going to cancel your order and mail you a $75.00 coupon if you choose to use our products in the future. I assure you that I will do a better job of managing my email, and I'm sorry for this inconvenience.

CUSTOMER: Okay. I appreciate your honesty, and we will see about the future. Thank you. (click)

I cannot promise Mrs. Jones will do business with Mike in the future. However, I can assure you that Mike handled the situation correctly. He also battled the **SBK** effect and gave himself every opportunity for future business. **Why?** Because he initiated the call and admitted his mistake with clarity, emphasis, sincerity, and some type of solution. If nothing else, my bet is that this potential lost customer will not bad mouth Mike because of how he handled himself. I'd put money on Mrs. Jones doing business with Morgan Blind Company in the future.

The practice of good **Customer Service** has been disappearing over the past few decades. The tools of the **SERVICE** trade have become rusty, and in some cases, have been thrown out altogether. Good **Core Values**, following the six MUST DO's and an honest, genuine approach to apologizing for your mistakes will carry your business far and keep your business healthy.

SERVICE TOOLS 138–163

138. **GET** to the customer before they get to you.

139. Tell the customer what they **DESERVE** to hear.

140. Deliver prompt **FOLLOW-UP**.

141. Deliver competent **FOLLOW-THROUGH**.

142. Use **PROFESSIONAL** words and attitude.

143. Learn **HOW** to say things with diligence and care.

144. Tune into the customer radio station **WIIFM**.

145. **VOLUNTEER** customer service information.

146. **ACKNOWLEDGE** receipt of email or phone inquiries.

147. Provide quality **RESPONSES** to email or phone inquiries.

148. **UPDATE** customers on your service efforts and results.

149. **CONFIRM** one-on-one conversations in writing.

150. Maintain a **WRITTEN** job trail, preferably email.

151. Avoid providing **SWIICFU** service.

152. Read customer orders **CAREFULLY** to avoid errors.

153. Leave call-back expectations on **VOICEMAIL** messages.

154. Install your **COMPANY NAME** on voicemail messages.

155. Know **HOW** you service leaves good or bad impressions.

156. Service customers with **TRUTH** and not smokescreens.

157. Realize that customers **DETECT** lies easily.

158. Be respectful and polite with customer **CARE**.

159. **MINIMIZE** customer involvement with service tasks.

160. Learn to **APOLOGIZE** quickly and emphatically.

161. Use **SINCERITY** when apologizing.

162. Pay attention to customer **BODY LANGUAGE**.

163. Learn to say **NO** politely.

Good COMMUNICATION demonstrates
respect for customer time and money.

TOOLS 164–201

SBK = Silent Business Killer

TALK • PHONE • VM • WRITE • EMAIL • TEXT • BLAST • SHARE • MESSAGE • POST • VLOG • BLOG • STREAM • TWEET • PODCAST

We have so many choices for how to communicate. What is the right way? What is the appropriate method? What is the wrong choice? The answer is simple for some small companies and complex for other business owners. Personally, I will provide time-tested feedback and sound suggestions based on what I have witnessed in my 75,000+ hours of situational business.

Each one of the methods in the opening of the chapter has a place. Their value, power and usefulness in growing business is unmistakable. My primary focus on **COMMUNICATION** will be the intimacy of business transactions between a company and a customer.

I am of the opinion that the state of **COMMUNICATION** within today's business atmosphere is borderline horrible! Instead of getting better as technology advances, a large portion of business **COMMUNICATION** (both internal and external) has morphed into a slow, lazy, messy mush of unanswered inquiries and cryptic responses that are often more confusing than helpful. Bottom line: In my opinion, professional business **COMMUNICATION** is at an all-time low. The small business owner community cannot afford to be part of or follow this trend.

Initiate or Respond

The way I see it, business ownership **COMMUNICATION** is a two-sided coin: initiate or respond. This part of running a business can be intimidating. Poor **COMMUNICATION** protocols can open the door to the dreaded **SBK**.

The CPA Writing Method

Initiating: In 1984–1987, I was calling on senior executives in the banking, brokerage, insurance and legal professions in the Wall Street area of New York City. Ninety-nine percent of these professionals had more business savvy and experience than I had in my left pinky finger! One of my jobs was to write letters to these people.

Writing letters was daunting and agonizing. However, in one Wednesday night sales meeting, our district manager covered this topic and introduced us to the **CPA** method of writing letters. The lightbulb went off! The intimidation and frustration disappeared. The veil of uncertainty was lifted. Writing letters got much easier. Communicating was simplified. **Why?** The answer lies in this three-letter memory trigger "**CPA**," not to be confused with the same term used for a certified public accountant.

Our district manager suggested we follow a simple road map of:

1) **Courtesy** – Say something simple and courteous.
2) **Purpose** – State why you are writing.
3) **Action** – Define what you want the reader to do.

With my head held high, I can tell you that I speak and write following this roadmap in 2019. I have been using it every day since 1985. When initiating a piece of business correspondence, simply approach it the way Mike would write to Mrs. Jones. (Remember Mike and Mrs. Jones from the **Service** chapter?)

Dear Mrs. Jones,

Hello and I hope you and your family are doing well. It is nice to finally say goodbye to that unusually cold winter we had this year.

The purpose of my note is to formally apologize for my mishandling of your order earlier this month. It is a terrible feeling to know I let you down with something so important. My hope is that your family get-together was a success and that you were able to find an adequate off-the-shelf blind replacement.

Please forgive me for my mistake, and consider giving me a second chance to provide blinds for other areas of your home. If given the chance again, I will do everything possible to exceed your expectations. Please accept this $75.00 coupon on your next order as my way of saying I'm sorry.

May you have continued success, and enjoy the nice weather!

Sincerely,

Mike Morgan, Morgan Blind Company

Simple and to the point! Mike followed the **CPA** roadmap and initiated a short, pertinent piece of correspondence. In fact, you may want to save this letter as a template for future use, a tip we will explore later in this chapter.

I make phone calls, write emails, leave voice messages and speak to people using this method. Thank you, Steve Arcoleo! This has been one of the most impactful business suggestions I have ever received. I have agonized over very few letters or correspondence since 1985.

Responding: Handling responses in customer-pleasing fashion
will continue to fortify healthy perceptions of your business. Processing responses haphazardly and lazily could contribute to issues pertaining to growth and financial strength. **Why?** Because this is where the **SBK** hovers, lurks and prowls. **SBKs** love when you don't manage **COMMUNICATION** properly. Lack of responding and low-quality responses are like seeds which sprout as weeds that squelch your business, limiting growth and customer retention.

Some American businesses are terrible at responding. Simply horrible. Several times each day, my inquiries go unanswered. For the past 20 years, I start my mornings by going backwards to push and pull for feedback to prior requests for information. Back-pedaling has become a daily task of resending unanswered inquiries from the day before, or many days before. I work for these companies, so I have to keep a level head and re-ask all these questions nicely and with a smile. Honestly, this is tiring and frustrating. It shows a lack of respect for my time and it is happening with alarming frequency.

If I was a customer being forced to push, pull and back-pedal to get responses, I'd look for vendors who show better respect for my time. Make sure you are on the right side of the fence managing responses to customers.

As I write these words, my current day started at 6:15 a.m. with the usual dose of poking and nudging to some of the brands I represent to give me feedback to unanswered questions. Six emails later I was almost ready to start forward motion, but I still had one more mission ahead of me.

My seventh little project while my morning was still in the reverse gear was to corral feedback to an important email now over 68 hours old. To wrestle a response from one of my VPs, I sent a text message to this executive the night before. The response to my text message was, "Call me in the morning." Now, the little voice in my head said, "Really...you can't just answer your email? Okay...you're the boss." So, at hour 68 I called him and finally got my answer.

We are not nearly done here! This course of events forced me to update my buyer. This note was letting her know my two-day-old inquiry had gone unanswered, and that I was calling my VP for an answer. In essence, it asked her to please stay tuned...I didn't forget about this issue...I am working on it. Here is the actual exchange:

From: Mason, Jeff
Sent: Wednesday, February 20, 2019 7:07 AM
To: Peggy
Subject: Jeff Mason - Question Update

Peggy,

Hello. I did not hear back from my VP yet, so I sent a text message to him. It doesn't sound like he read my email from Monday. I will call him in about one hour to try and get an answer. Stay tuned!

Best Regards,

Jeff Mason

From: Peggy
Sent: Wednesday, February 20, 2019 7:09 AM
To: Mason, Jeff
Subject: RE: Jeff Mason - Question Update

I appreciate you. Thank you so much!

Did you notice her response? **"I appreciate you."**

My point in illustrating this is the following:

COMMUNICATION is hard work to do the right way. However, customers respond favorably when you communicate effectively. Consumers like being looped-in. Clients gravitate to doing business with companies that respect their time. **"I appreciate you"** says a lot in those three little words. My buyer didn't have to pester me, and she doesn't have to worry about my watching her wallet. Peggy knows that I am a vendor rep who she can count on. Her encouraging response gives me comfort. **Why?** When I read between the lines, Peggy is telegraphing me that she is okay with my effort, and that she and her company are spending their money in the right place. Peggy will keep giving me business because she knows I have her back. She knows I am doing the tedious legwork that makes her job easier. By the way, my email to Peggy is a form of what I call "**Courtesy Communication.**"

❖ KEY COMMUNICATION TIP

Don't make your customers back-pedal to get answers from you.

Remember my story in the **Service** chapter...46 days...42 emails and six phone calls just to answer two customer questions. Sadly, these scenarios take place all too often, and they have been growing in frequency over the past two decades. Customers don't tolerate this. They flee and rarely come back because the **SBK** hits hard.

The good news for bigger companies is that they can financially weather these storms brought on by bad communicators. The bad news for us small companies: We take a huge financial hit quickly if we stink at responding. We don't have the financial strength to outlast poor **COMMUNICATION**. When a customer fires us, or we lose a potential job, the impact of that loss is much heavier on us than a large company that can absorb it more easily. You cannot afford to let your dream slip away because you are bad at communicating. Execute responses properly and protect the precious time, energy and money you devoted to building your company.

If you follow these proven and tested suggestions for responding, it will be easier for your business to remain healthy and grow. You will look and feel refreshingly exciting. Don't forget, there is so much bad **COMMUNICATION** in the business world that customers are not exposed to a daily diet of good communicators. Your professionalism will be a welcomed change.

This customer excitement will assist in spreading the news about your reputation. Word of mouth will aid your business in coffee shop conversations, social media posts, restaurant gatherings and family events. Your phone will ring a little more...your email will bring a little more...and your text messages will ding a little more!

Courtesy Communication

I love **Courtesy Communication (C-COM)**. I once suggested it to one of my VPs, and he just laughed at me. "Not gonna happen" was his response. Not many people do this because the perception is that it takes too much time. The reality is that 90% of **C-COM** will be two or three sentences that take 60–90 seconds to write. **C-COM** can be used in various types of interactions. The most common business situation to deploy **C-COM** is rooted in a customer inquiry. I use the memory trigger **"ARU"** to guide me on this type of **C-COM**:

- **Acknowledge** email/phone call/voice message.
- **Respond** with anticipated timeline of next correspondence.
- **Update** periodically, independent of customer prompting.

This simple formula will keep you on task and will deliver a consistent pattern of processing business. **ARU** is one of my hallmarks and separates me from many of my competitors.

What does C-COM do for a customer?

The valuable and money-making foundation of **Courtesy Communication** is "getting to your customer before they get to you." In essence, the consistent use of **C-COM** enables you to be one step ahead of your client. This discipline is advantageous to customers in the following ways:

• answers a question that is probably top of mind,
• provides an answer before a question is asked of you,
• establishes buying confidence,
• creates and sustains long-term trust,
• enhances perception that you are taking care of their money,
• demonstrates that you value the business partnerships, and
• enables you to create and deliver on expectation timelines.

What does C-COM do for a team member?

Suppliers, associates, sub-contractors and manufacturers (team members) will genuinely appreciate **Courtesy Communication**. Consider this small example as proof.

In advance, I send out vacation notifications to all the companies for whom I work. In 2008, a Chief Executive Officer called me minutes after receiving one of these emails from me. He was shocked. Paraphrasing his response, in all his years running the company I was the first independent manufacturing representative to ever send a vacation notice. In this phone call he went on to tell me that most of time he cannot even get his independent reps to respond to his calls and emails. My simple and proactive **C-COM** knocked him off his chair.

I no longer work for this manufacturer, but we still bump into each other at industry trade shows. To this day he tells me I am the best rep that ever worked for him. **Why?** The answer is **C-COM**. Was I actually the best rep to ever work for this person? Absolutely not! However, the impression I left with that simple 2008 vacation notification created an unshakeable, positive perception with that CEO that will be glued to me for the rest of my career. You want to create these perceptions too, as they are healthy for your business and long-term return on investment of time and money.

Quality **C-COM** will benefit your operating support cast in the following ways:

- shows you value their partnership,
- demonstrates you respect their time,
- answers questions they are thinking about,
- paves the way for a stronger partnership,
- enable your partners to do a better, faster job,
- prevents task duplication by other partner associates, and
- helps everyone to be more up-to-date and informed.

C-COM Example Emails

Team Member UNSOLICITED Update

From: Jeff Mason
Sent: Wednesday, February 01, 2012 4:47 PM
To: "SARAH"
Subject: PD LOGO ITEMS - NEW CUSTOMER – 1/26/12
Importance: High

Sarah,

Good afternoon. Matt left me a voice message telling me that the order is forthcoming. The delay on the order is because they could not get it in time for Christmas. They are still committed but cannot determine the correct finish. We should have something within 2-6 weeks.

Thanks for your patience.

Jeff Mason

Customer ORDER ACKNOWLEDGMENT

-----Original Message-----
From: Jeff Mason
Sent: Monday, February 27, 2012 7:07 AM
To: "JOYCE"
Subject: PURCHASE ORDER NUMBER 05833182

Joyce,

Thank you. We are processing now. Have a good day.

Best Regards,

Jeff Mason

Team Member THANK YOU

From: Jeff Mason
Sent: Thursday, March 08, 2012 2:17 PM
To: "SARAH"
Subject: DROP BOXES - MASON THANK YOU - 3/8/12

Sarah,

Thank you for sending the Drop Boxes to Tyler. I really appreciate it. Have a nice day.

Jeff Mason

Customer INQUIRY – Part One

From: Linda
Sent: Friday, March 09, 2012 9:29 AM
To: Jeff Mason
Subject: Update Needed on Past Due Orders

Good morning - I show the following order are past due. Can you advise if these orders have shipped (PO: 5658263 & PO: 5726838)? If so, can I get the tracking number? If it has not shipped, can you advise when it will ship?

I also show the following order (PO: 5766775) that is due here next week. Can you advise if this item has shipped? If not, can you advise when it is scheduled to ship?

Linda
Buyer

Customer INQUIRY – Part Two

From: Jeff Mason
Sent: Friday, March 09, 2012 9:41 AM
To: Linda
Subject: Update Needed on Past Due Orders

Linda,

I'm looking into it now and should have feedback later today.

Best Regards,

Jeff Mason

RWIICFM
(Respond When It Is Convenient For Me)

Don't fall into this trap. It will kill your business. I know, it is tempting because you operate your own company, and you call the shots. Well, even though this attitude is on the rise, don't see it and fall for it.

What do I mean it is on the rise? I get more and more emails that state something to this effect: "Thank you for contacting me. I am out of the office on business for the next three weeks. Contact my assistant if you have any questions." SERIOUSLY? No, really...SERIOUSLY? Companies allow key personnel to not answer emails for three weeks while they are out of the office? Shame on those executives for letting this happen. Do their investors know this? Do the major shareholders know this?

If you are a major shareholder of a company, ask the question at your next board meeting. Then, just to double check on your own, send a group email out to all the department heads that night and see what type of automated responses you get. *BRACE YOURSELF!*

You and I cannot afford to inconvenience one customer or potential customer. Not one! Remember your loan, or inheritance, or the 401K you wiped clean, or years of savings you used to start your company. Like I said, you need to answer every business email, voice message or text rapidly. We may have different definitions of rapid. I choose to respond within a few minutes and not to exceed eight hours. An associate of mine (Randy) was taught the "sundown" policy by a bank. Simply stated: Answer the customer by sundown that day. Create your own timeline policy and adhere to it with consistency.

Go back to the **Expectations** and **Core Values** you created. Remind yourself of what you said you would do. Stick to your credos, and execute timely responses.

I have averaged 99 nights per year in hotels for the last five years. I assure you, each and every night, or at the crack of dawn the next morning, I tackle my email inbox. I let nothing...I mean zero correspondence...go unanswered or unacted upon before I head out for my daily appointments. I do this every day, without fail. **Why?** Because I invested thousands to start my dream and I aim to get a good return on that investment. If I lose a customer, it won't be for a lack of trying. I will do whatever it takes, and it starts with answering their questions and concerns ASAP.

What to Avoid When Writing Business Communications

Knowledge is power. Chances are, you are well versed in your industry and most certainly the products and services you provide. Don't assume your customers have even 20% of the knowledge you do. Be careful of projecting your knowledge as being superior to that of your customers. If you do, and many business people do, you run the high risk of alienating your customers and opening the door for **SBKs**.

In addition to coming off as a know-it-all, steer clear of other simple **COMMUNICATION** *no-no's:*

- *Arrogance*
- *Sarcasm*
- *Dishonesty*

Additional items to avoid:

- *Industry jargon*
- *Industry acronyms*
- *Political commentary*

Stock Letters/Emails

This is a very useful system to implement. It may seem a little old school...but then again, sometimes traditional is still functional and easy. Creating these internal libraries of boilerplate correspondence saves you time and increases efficiency and productivity. It simply works to identify which saved letter or email you need, then grab it, change a few variables, save, print and/or hit "Send."

Six Easy Set-Up Steps

1) Create and save each document type on your computer.
2) Save it to another shared drive.
3) Print a copy of the letter or email.
4) Write the file name on the printed copy.
5) Store the 8.5" x11" document in a three-ring binder.
6) Keep the binder in an accessible spot or shelf.

Suggestion: Review documents from time to time. Chances are you will recognize some words or sentences to change. It will improve your next mailings.

Suggested Stock Letters/Emails

ANNUAL CHECK-UP/POST JOB COMPLETION
ANNUAL PRICE CHANGE
APOLOGY- LATE DELIVERY
APOLOGY- ORDER ENTRY ERROR
CATALOG (electronic version/email)
CATALOG mailing letter
DISCONTINUED ITEMS
INTRODUCTION
JOB COMPLETION/THANK YOU
MEETING CONFIRMATION
MEETING/THANK YOU
PHONE CALL DISCUSSION/THANK YOU
PRE-SEASON BUYS
QUOTE
SERVICE RENDERED/THANK YOU
SIX MONTH CHECK-UP/POST JOB COMPLETION
SPECIAL PROMOTION

Email Only

HOLIDAY CLOSURE
OFFICE CLOSURE
ORDER CONFIRMATION (You can set this up as a signature.)
VOICE MESSAGE FOLLOW-UP

Repurpose Sent Emails

This is another valuable trick of the trade, very similar to STOCK LETTERS & EMAILS. They are cousins. A VP of Sales made a comment to me back in 2010: "Mason, I have never seen anyone produce such a volume of information in such a short period of time as you. I know what you do for our brand; I can only imagine what you do for all the brands you work for. How do you pull it off?"

The answer was easy. I repurpose old ("Sent") emails to save time. In other words, once I finish sending the "2018 NEW PRICING" email, I store all the Sent copies in an electronic file cabinet. Then, when 2019 rolls around, I grab the files, double check to make sure all links are active, and change the date and any relevant messaging. Promotions, item discontinuations, new products, excess inventory and holiday emails all get reused to save me time.

I don't deal with hundreds and hundreds of customers per brand I represent. In most cases, I deal with dozens and dozens. As a result, I tend to shy away from GROUP EMAIL BLASTS. I choose to send each email out separately to each account. Often times I will start these emails in a conversational manner that pertains to their personal life (kids, local weather, alma mater, vacations etc.). I like to give each release a personal finesse rather than the colder feeling where every customer is lumped together in the notification. Because of my personalized style, repurposed emails pay me huge dividends.

The reality is that many of my competitors choose not to send these personal emails. Instead, they opt for a generic approach, bundling their email contact list into a one-touch sending event. This does save time, and I am all for that with certain updates. However, for the most part, grouping all clients together creates a missed opportunity for a personal connection with customers. I move quickly, cover a lot of ground and could not do so without the ability to repurpose previously written emails.

Mistake Warning: With the repurposing of old emails comes a higher degree of error potential. My two most common are:

Mistake #1:

A. I just sent an email to my buyer named Jane.
B. Then I retrieve it out of "Sent" emails to repurpose.
C. I make it out to Bob, hit send and it still says "Dear Jane."

Mistake #2:

A. I grab my old "2017 Holiday Specials" to use for 2018.
B. I change the date range to reflect 2018 dates.
C. I start sending but the subject reads "2017 Holiday Specials."

Yep! I make my share of silly mistakes for sure. So, learn from me and try to be extra careful when you repurpose emails. When I make these mistakes I follow up with another email that contains an apology, the corrections and an explanation of what I did wrong. It takes extra time, but the customer deserves a revision and a brief summary why they are receiving the updated correspondence.

Face-To-Face Communications

Talking with potential and current customers is essential in many businesses but not all. For example, I have booked 450 nights with this same discount hotel broker and have only spoken to them on two occasions. Another example is the editor of this book. To date we have never spoken, yet we communicate regularly and effectively through email.

First, please put yourself in the position of the listener before you begin to speak. Speak to your potential or current customers in a manner you would want to be spoken to. It is not what you say as much as how you say it. My wife always tells me that, and it's true. People will size you up in many ways, but one of them is how you say things. Are you condescending, are you a know-it-all, do you interrupt, do you embellish stories? Be conscientious and learn to be deliberate, respectful and professional in your speaking manner.

Secondly, people are trained through life experiences to look for what is wrong. They become accustomed to reading between the lines. You should not embellish, boast and lie to get business. Customers can smell dishonesty when they get near it. You are not fooling anyone. The **SBK** feasts in these environments, and you are probably losing **Repeat** and/or **Referral Customers** without recognizing the menacing and unseen force working against you. If you operate this way, I strongly urge you to stop the mistruths, embellishments and arrogant boasting today because they will sink you.

141

Consider this analogy. At the core of law enforcement is a mix of proactive and reactive responsibilities. In both cases, the goal is to seek out and establish the truth. Law enforcement personnel learn to read between the lines when assessing a situation. They usually evaluate input with one skeptical eyebrow up while combing through the details. They are trained to look at a situation and detect what the naked eye cannot see. They read body language, observe surroundings and spot clues that neither you nor I ever see. So much of what they hear and process is false that, over time, they develop a skill for identifying lies on their way to finding the truth.

My buddy, "Jimmy the H," is a retired law enforcement professional of 20 years. He can sense a lie in 15-30 seconds during a face-to-face discussion. I've personally witnessed Jimmy's knack for spotting mistruths on numerous occasions. It's amazing! His quick and blunt response: "Put a fork in that story. It's done." Someone will rarely win him back after the fork is in their story.

Customers are the same way. They have heard all the tricks in the book. They smell fibs, little white lies and tall tales a mile away. They have been there, done that. When they know you are spreading the lie (like peanut butter on bread), they listen politely, say thank you and game over...drop the microphone! When their door closes behind you, you are done. Put a fork in it. Then, here comes your old nemesis, the **SBK** effect.

Speak truth, and do so in a professional manner. This is a win-win combination. Pure and simple!

Be Conversational & Smile

Just be yourself. Relax. Without diving into sales training, your best option is to be you and present what you do in a natural, normal speaking manner. Smiling will help to set a positive tone and energize the relationship-building process. Learn to look people in the eye when you talk. Direct eye contact will assist in creating positive first impressions and pave the road to earning customer trust. Be humble, avoid lying, and put a comfortable 18" distance between you and the buyer. Use your **Proof/Evidence Portfolio**, provide them with your **Expectation List**, and let your follow-up and follow-through win them over.

Read the Room

When you first meet a potential client, be sure to smile widely then thank them for their time. The opening question I ask is the following: "I know you are very busy, so please let me know how much time we have for this meeting?"

If a client allocates 20 minutes, you better not tell stories for 15 minutes. Ask good questions and start sharing, showing, telling, and selling yourself with your **Evidence Portfolio**. Keep looking around at the folks in the room. Are they rolling their eyes? Are they getting overly anxious or looking at their watches, texting or going on social media? If I sense uneasiness or apprehension, I suggest pulling out this old school move. Take out your cellphone or take off your watch, place it on the table and say, "Okay, I'll put that right here, front and center. This way we can both see it and make sure we don't go over 20 minutes."

Then, pick up the pace and get the show on the road. My guess is most audiences will chuckle and start liking you a little bit more.

Example

I was with a VP of Sales in a high-profile sale call. We were already doing Men's business, and now the Women's buyers wanted our line. It was pretty much a done deal, and I was able to handle the appointment by myself. However, this executive insisted on flying out for the meeting.

Cutting to the chase...the VP had a computer malfunction in the middle of this extremely boring PowerPoint slideshow. The presentation was in the front of the room, the buyers were in the middle of the room, and I was to the side of the buyers. This technology glitch stretched on and on. One minute turned into two, then three minutes. Finally, the VP said, "I'll just reboot my computer and start over." I cringed at this plan because I was already reading the room, and it was not good.

Upon hearing the news of 'rebooting' the computer, the three buyers gradually began to writhe and reposition their bodies in their chairs. They started sliding, squirming and fidgeting. They turned their heads to each other as all sets of eyes rolled, heads flung backwards, and arms flailed in the air. I finally got up and took over the meeting as I knew the bleeding had to stop. To this day, I have never been invited back to step foot in the corporate headquarters. The company stopped doing business with me just one year after this meeting. Here is the sad part: This executive was oblivious to all the buyer angst and frustration. I never had the heart to inform the VP what transpired. The lesson of this 100% true story: **Read the room!**

Take Good Notes

There is no right or wrong way for taking meeting notes. The important thing is to make sure you record specifics very carefully. Quality information is your insurance policy that protects your profitability.

I prefer to use leather journals, and I file them for safekeeping when they are full. I have retained all my note journals since I started my sales agency in 2008. (See the picture below.) This is a sound approach to capture the meeting details and retain the information for long periods of time. This eliminates the dreaded loss of single sheet notes that mysteriously vanish from our grasp. I have gone back into these notebooks on many occasions to review entries such as specifications, names, numbers and timelines. Accurate and detailed information leads to effective **COMMUNICATION.**

What to Avoid When Meeting Face-To-Face

- *Being a chronic INTERRUPTER.*
- *Being a chronic CORRECTOR.*
- *Displaying ARROGANCE.*
- *BRAGGING.*
- *Using EMBELLISMENTS.*
- *Acting SUPERIOR over customers.*
- *Speaking in a CONDESCENDING manner.*
- *Using industry SLANG or terms.*
- *Making EMPTY CLAIMS you cannot support.*
- *SKIPPING OVER customer questions.*
- *VIOLATING social space.*
- *Taking PHONE CALLS.*
- *TEXTING other people.*
- *OVERPROMISING capabilities or timelines.*
- *MOCKING & KNOCKING your competition.*
- *BAD MOUTHING neighbors or other customers.*
- *Eating ONIONS prior to your meeting.*
- *Entering homes with MUDDY feet.*
- *Bringing open BEVERAGES into a private residence.*

COMMUNICATION TOOLS 164–201

164. Answer **100%** of inquiries you receive.

165. Respond to inquiries in a **TIMELY** manner.

166. Read all electronic **ATTACHMENTS** carefully.

167. Read the **ENTIRE** email that is sent with attachments.

168. Answer questions with **DIRECT** responses.

169. Provide **COURTESY COMMUNICATION (C-COM).**

170. Remove anxiety by using the CPA method when **WRITING.**

171. Remove anxiety by using the CPA method when **TALKING.**

172. Think like the **READER** when writing emails and letters.

173. Express **CONFIDENCE** (not arrogance).

174. Demonstrate **SINCERITY.**

175. Write **CLEARLY.**

176. Use **SIMPLE** words when writing.

177. Explain **WHY** in your correspondence.

178. Use the word **WE** in place of I.

179. Number **REQUESTS & QUESTIONS.**

180. List **DATES** in completion/delivery correspondence.

181. Name **CARRIERS** (USPS/UPS/FED EX) & **TRACKING** #s.

182. Fully **DESCRIBE** revisions and changes.

183. List **ITEM #s** on correspondence and in marketing.

184. Write emails with mission-specific **SUBJECT** titles.

185. **SEGMENT** different topics in singular correspondence.

186. Send **MEETING RECAPS** after meetings and discussions.

187. Erase internal email trails before **FORWARDING** externally.

188. Write **COMPREHENSIVE** emails to reduce future questions.

189. **OMIT** opinion in business social media posts.

190. Use social media accounts **WISELY** and **RESPONSIBLY.**

191. **HEAR** what customers are saying.

192. **LISTEN** to what customers are saying.

193. Learn to sincerely **SMILE** face-to-face or on the phone.

194. Make consistent **EYE CONTACT** in face-to-face meetings.

195. Organize electronic information by **TOPIC** or **CUSTOMER.**

196. **SAVE** important sent emails in electronic files.

197. **REPURPOSE** announcement or marketing emails.

198. Practice **REVISING** critical emails before releasing.

199. Save critical emails **OVERNIGHT** for next day perspective.

200. **RELEASE** final, critical emails in mornings for sharpness.

201. Include **CONTACT** information in electronic signatures.

"In business, you want to manage
and control the elements of the business
itself, not the numbers on your profit-and-loss
statement. The numbers are there to reflect how
well or how poorly your business is doing."

Harold Geneen and Alvin Moscow, *Managing* (1984)

TOOLS 202–233

SBK = Silent Business Killer

Pennies over Dollars

In my career I have come to conclude, it is not the big DOLLARS that matter as much as the pennies, nickels, dimes and quarters. **Why?** *Because when it comes to losing hard-earned profits, it is the disappearance of those small coins that, over time, lead to the DOLLARS.* You can minimize the loss of sizeable profit if you focus on the smaller, quiet, hard-to-see, slow and sneaky financial calamities that collectively add up to and cripple or close many small businesses.

Let's do a quick rewind to the **Procedure** chapter.

Handful of Sand

When and if you visit the beach, try this simple exercise: Grab a handful of dry sand (the finer the sand, the better), tightly clench your hand and bring your closed fist up to your eye level. For the next few seconds, watch the tiny crystals fall out of your grasp and land on the ground. Those scattered particles represent coins (pennies, nickels, dimes and quarters) that quietly disappear from your business. This lost money diminishes the financial success of your business. Hold on to your sand!

Harold Geneen summed it up so well in the opening quote. What he is really saying is this: Don't fiddle or change your numbers on a profit and loss statement. Your profits and losses on the statement are like a mirror; they are a reflection of your business condition. If the numbers are bad, that means they are indicating something is wrong with the way you are running your business. The problem is NOT the numbers. If you want to fix or change the numbers, then change the way you are doing business.

My goal in this section is not to be a financial advisor. My objective is to highlight simple concepts to help your business retain more profit and assist in keeping your small business ownership dream alive. Please know that **Procedures** are vitally connected to the financial condition and health of your company. Additionally, **Details**, **Margin Erosion** and **Variances** are intertwined and also tethered to the financial posture of your business.

Doctor of Details

This cannot be stressed enough. **Details** matter more than we give them credit for. Being **Detail-oriented** is hard. I won't kid you — it takes diligence and focus to be good at **Detail Management**. It's not fun. It's tedious and time consuming. However, it is a must if you plan on being profitable and sustaining long-term small business ownership. You must commit to managing **Details**.

The cost can be high when you do not focus on **Details**. Consider some observations I have witnessed in my career that resulted in lost profitability due to carelessness.

- Invoices never sent for completed jobs.
- Customers asking for vendor invoices to be sent.
- Power tools being left behind after the completion of a job.
- Contractor equipment left in the rain to rust and ruin.
- Multiple, daily packages sent to same international address.
- $500 monthly data line charge paid over years for no reason.
- Office heat set at 74 degrees over weekends (good for mice).
- Sample room set at 55 degrees year-round.

I could go on and on and on. I have encountered so many instances where profitability dribbles out of a company…and the company never knew about it until it was too late to recoup the losses.

Let's unpack four of the examples I mentioned to illustrate the cost of being poor at **Detail Management**.

Invoices Never Sent

a) I received a quote for a $600 home repair in April 2015.
b) The job was completed in mid-June.
c) 30 days went by, and I never received an invoice.
d) Mid-July, I called the business owner.
e) Mid-August and still no return call from business owner.
f) Mid-August, I called again. No return call.
g) Mid-September, still no invoice received.
h) Mid-September, I sent a copy of owner quote to owner. (My message: "Please send me an invoice.")
i) Early-October I got an invoice which I paid on 10/9/15.
j) Look below at the note the business owner wrote me. (*"I'm not sure what happened!"*) Hmmm!

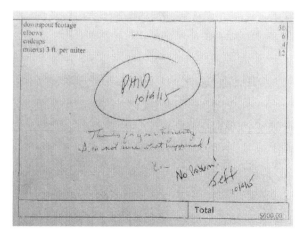

Lost Profitability: Most of the job was labor. However, at least $100–$150 went toward specific parts that were acquired to complete the job. Almost 115 days went by before this owner was reimbursed for parts he purchased in mid-June. The sad reality is this: I had to pester the business owner so he could get paid. His loss is hard to calculate. I am certain that this business cannot thrive very long if even 50% of customer payments take 115 days like this example.

Asking Vendor to Send Invoices

a) Since 2015, my yard received nine monthly treatments.
b) Many, many invoices were inaccurate and needed correction.
c) Service provider developed a pro-rated invoicing system.
d) Invoices are to be emailed by the 15th of each month.

Consider this email:

From: Mason, Jeff
Sent: Tuesday, May 15, 2018 8:36 AM
To: Administration
Cc: Business Owner
Subject: Jeff Mason - 2018 SERVICE

Dear Service Provider,

Hello. It has been 70 days since I received an invoice. To date I have only paid 1 of 9 installments for service this year. To date I have received 2 rounds of service.

Are you still with _ _ _ _ _? If so, please send me invoice #2.

Please advise the cadence of invoices?

Best Regards,

Jeff Mason

Lost Profitability: Invoices are to be sent every 30 days. I paid the first in the beginning of March. 70 days had gone by without another invoice, yet I had received two rounds of yard treatment. The reality is this: I had to press them so they could collect money from me. How many other customers just say, "The heck with it, if they don't send me an invoice, it's their problem not mine." I can't even do the math on this one. Who knows how deep and wide the invoicing problems run? For three years I spent too much time and energy asking for invoices and chasing down information. I finally parted ways with this service in 2019.

Inflated International Package Costs

a) I worked for a company with three international offices.
b) Our USA office sent multiple, daily packages internationally.
c) International offices sent multiple, daily packages to USA.
d) Our USA office paid outbound-inbound freight charges.
e) Finally, someone did a cost analysis (years later).
f) We corrected the process two-fold:
  1) The company started grouping packages together.
  2) The company began sending/receiving twice per week.
g) The changes resulted in saving over $120,000 annually.

Lost Profitability: Probably $120,000 for many, many years! We were an eight-million-dollar company spending over $170,000 annually on international merchandising packages within our own company. *UGLY!*

Monthly Dormant Data Line Charge

a) I worked for a USA company with an office in Puerto Rico.
b) Our USA office conducted an "outgoing check audit."
c) Our CEO reviewed every check before we mailed it.
d) The purpose of this exercise was to spend money wisely.
e) We discovered a $500 monthly fee for a dormant data line.
   1) Line connected our USA office and our Puerto Rico office.
f) We were paying for this dormant line for many, many years.

Lost Profitability: We wasted somewhere between $18,000 and $24,000 over the long haul. I thought the check audit was a little over the top when I first heard we were going to do it. However, I was clearly wrong. This check auditing exercise enabled us to catch and eliminate many other unnecessary expenditures that we did without from that day forward.

Standard Operating Procedures

Standard Operating Procedures (SOPs) are beneficial disciplines to assist your business in establishing structure and a repetitive operational framework. **SOPs** also create a good system for measuring performance against a set standard. For example, if you can measure and monitor the true cost of all business components, it is easier to manage their profitability. Standardizing procedures assists in this measurement-management relationship.

Revisit the **Procedure** chapter to support some of the following discussion points.

Variances

Margin Erosion and **Variances** are directly related. Consider this simplified explanation:

• **Margin Erosion** is the unplanned loss of profitability.
• **Variances** are the result from **Margin Erosion** events.

Variances are created from unexpected changes to actual costs that alter margin structure. In a simplified example, you think you are making $12.50 profit on the sale of your product, but after actual **Variances** are calculated, you only make $9.37 profit. The real enemy here is not being able to identify and understand what happened to the $3.13 of profit that disappeared.

Please embrace grasping these occurrences because this is where pennies really add up. *Most importantly, **Variances** are usually self-inflicted due to absent or poor procedural protocols.* (See *DAMAGE TRACER* below.)

This is another huge partner of the **SBK**. In most cases, we overlook **Variances** and many companies never record them. The difference between estimated costs and actual costs derive from those classic 'grains of sand' that escape through our clenched fists. You must wrap your arms around this in your business. When you put all of this together, **Details**, **Margin Erosion** and **Variances** are interrelated and glued to the financial disposition of your company.

Tree Service Variances

(We will use a real-life tree service situation I referenced in the **Procedure** chapter.)

DAMAGE TRACER: All this financial pain and stifled potential growth is the direct result of this company not measuring my fence opening at the time of the job quote.

1) Day 12 — time to prepare, load, deploy and return truck.
2) Day 12 — gas used in truck for roundtrip #1.
3) Day 12 — loss of billable time on another paying job.
4) Day 56 — loss of billable time on another paying job.
5) Day 56 — time to prepare, load, deploy and return truck.
6) Day 56 — gas used in truck for roundtrip #2.
7) Day 56 — rental cost for stump grinder.
8) Day 87 — final $75.00 was still uncollected.
9) Day 88 — final $75.00 was voluntarily mailed.

Transaction Variances & Loss: My estimate for the total loss of this $425.00 job is $125.00 at a minimum. This takes into account the $75.00 I voluntarily sent on Day 88. This is a devastating 29.4% loss off the total job cost. Furthermore, this $125.00 loss is the majority of the profit this business owner expected to make from the job. Here is where this story gets sad.

- This tree service company was *referred* by a satisfied friend.
- I had to push and nudge to get service completed (56 days).
- The company lost a large chunk of profit.

- The company did not earn our endorsement.
- The **SBK** prevailed by preventing our *referral.*

Summary: Real profits can vary compared to estimated costs if you don't manage the **Details**. Wrapping your arms around actual cost tracking and instituting sound **Procedures** will guide and assist you in realizing a healthy financial condition.

Gross Profit & Markups

These are frequently used terms and helpful for **Money** management. Banks, accountants and investors also use these equations to measure financial performance and business health. In the below examples Revenue (R) is your Selling Price.

Gross Profit	Revenue	Cost	Profit
P = R minus C	$12.00	$8.00	$4.00

Gross Profit Margin (%)	Profit	Revenue	GPM %
GPM = P divided by R	$4.00	$12.00	33%

Markup (%)	Profit	Cost	MU %
MU = P divided by C	$4.00	$8.00	50%

Annual Work Computations
For Your Forecasting/Projection Purposes

- There are six major holiday closures.
- The average worker takes two weeks of vacation time.
- The average worker takes five days of personal time off (PTO).
- There are 52 weekends (104 days).
- The average business year is 240 days.
- 240 days = 365 minus 6 minus 104 minus 10 minus 5.

Measuring & Managing

Financially sound business operators usually adopt air-tight practices of measuring all the expenses associated with operating the business, producing the products and/or delivering the services. If you cannot measure these business costs, it will be hard to manage them and realize maximum profitability.

Measuring Example – My Hotel Expenses

In the second year of my agency, I was beginning to rack up the hotel stays. When I did my year-end taxes, I discovered that I was spending an average of $102.00 per night (including tax) for my hotels. In addition, the hotels I used were modestly rated at between 2.0 and 2.5 stars. **I knew I had to bring my hotel expenses down.** I decided to try using discount hotel brokers.

I was successful, and I have never turned back. My costs went well below $100 per night for the past eight years. I used one service for two years and switched to a better service for the past six plus years. My stats for the past five years are 494 nights at total cost of $46,170.46. Two things happened when I made this switch:

1. My average cost went down 8.4% to $93.46 per night.
2. Hotel star rating went from 2–2.5 all the way to a 3–3.5.

The net/net result: **I lowered my price 8.4% and raised the quality of my hotel stays**. Since I pay for hotels out of my pocket, it is advantageous for me to measure and manage this process and gain a favorable outcome on price and quality. This is huge for me as I was able to lower my annual out-of-pocket costs by $854 per year. In addition, booking travel is easy, user-friendly and speedy which conserves my time and saves me additional **MONEY** (although hard to quantify).

My First Company
Failure at Measuring & Managing

My father and I went into business in 1988. Dad did his due diligence, and he opened a franchise specializing in laser printer toner cartridge remanufacturing. He entered into a high-interest, $200,000+ home equity loan, and the two of us launched into business. All the financial forecasts and projections were built on the premise of $69.00 per unit for the selling price. Our franchise headquarters was in Iowa, and this $69.00 price was a national average. Off we went into the great NYC Metro area at $69.00 per unit.

Yikes! Guess what we missed? The average sell price per unit in the NYC Metro market was $42.00. What, a $27.00 difference in the average selling price? Yep. Put a fork in us! We were done in two years. I had built up a decent base of customers in that time period, so I left the business to my dad who limped, kicked and scraped for the next 14 years until he finally retired the next-to-nothing business.

That is what happens when you fail to effectively measure and manage! *Lesson learned!*

Miniature Management

This is another modern-day trap that I urge you to avoid to save more of your hard-earned profitability. It is very tempting to operate your company from a smartphone. I'm sure there are some pretty sharp business owners who can pull it off. However, it is so challenging to run day-to-day operations off a hand-held device that most of us will make costly mistakes if we do so.

Personally, I have made my share of minor errors when using my smartphone. These mistakes are irritating because they contradict my commitment to *detail* and *accuracy*. Mobile device technology tends to format information a little differently than laptops and office computers. The smaller information windows can easily cause even the best of us to miss some critical data that requires our careful attention.

There is a time and place for hand-held mobile technology as it is enormously beneficial when we are away from the office. My suggestion is to give thoughtful review to where and to what extent you will use a mobile product in place of your bigger screen computers.

When **MONEY**, critical decisions, specifications or spreadsheet analysis is required, please consider using your laptop, tablet or office computer. BIG SCOPE management oversight deserves our most comprehensive business equipment. In my opinion, miniature screen technology limits our ability to see everything with the *clarity* and *focus* necessary to weigh detailed business information. The last thing you need to do is lose a customer, a deal, or make a terrible financial decision because you missed something due to the formatting of a smartphone.

Lastly, know when to use text messaging and when not to. One VP I work with rarely answers an email. However, this executive almost always rapidly answers a text message. Okay, I applaud the speed of answering quickly, but I don't agree with the decision to ignore emails in favor of text messages. Trust me, someday when that individual needs an email trail (**Evidence D-E-F-E-A-T-S Disbelief**), he will have nothing because his text messages will be wiped clean. No evidence or track record will exist to support the business battle that requires a hard copy. There is a place and time for texting.

In the event you receive or send decision-oriented text messages, please email screenshots of these to your customers and copy yourself. This will allow you to retain a hard copy trail and fortify your evidence files in case a decision is contended days, weeks or months later.

Touch Things Once
Management Efficiency

This simple directive changed many things for me. As small business operators, we move fast, wear many hats and must be efficient with our use of time. Many years ago I heard someone say, "Touch things once." The lightbulb went off. The example given was opening mail and processing it immediately, instead of opening it all then putting it to the side to be acted on at a later time.

When my head hits the pillow, I have five, ten or fifteen things on my plate every single night. Seriously, since 2008, to do my job the way it needs to be done, I have that many daily projects and duties on my to-do list when I turn in for the evening. I am sure many readers can relate.

❖ KEY EFFICIENCY TIP
*Don't keep looking at it...*open it, process it, save it, send it, file it, discard it or forward it.

It's Your Money

Always take the time to remind yourself why you are in business. Remember how much it cost you and your family to start the business. Don't throw all that **MONEY** and toil away due to sloppiness or a "shoot from the hip" approach.

This book is all about your **MONEY.** My desire is to help you and your families receive the best return possible on the resources devoted to establishing and growing the business. The **Tools** in this book point directly to that outcome.

I periodically recall that my initial cost was $12,000 to start my company in 2008. I used the combination of a credit card at 11% interest and a credit union personal access loan at 8% interest. More importantly, it has cost far greater than $12,000 to grow my company and get past the first five years. I was fortunate. Regardless of how you finance your company, you are a risk taker who is looking for a favorable return on your investment of time and **MONEY**.

If you can afford it, I strongly suggest you get some professional help to teach you how to identify and quantify the real cost of doing business. This does not require a massive annual expenditure. I discovered a way to run my business and track my expenses with accounting assistance from a CPA for around $900 annually. That is it…$900 each year. The first time I sent my tax summary to my accountant, he called me and said, "Can I use this to show other small business owners how to track their expenses? This is well done, Jeff."

All I did was use Excel, do weekly expense reports, itemize my operating expenses and save my receipts. The rest takes care of itself. There are plenty of off-the-shelf bookkeeping and tax software programs for small business you can purchase if you are comfortable doing your taxes without an accountant.

We will cover expense tracking in podcasts starting in late 2019. Please visit **www.simplebiz360.com** for podcast details.

Do-It Yourself (DIY) Websites

In 2008, I hired a friend to create and maintain my website for around $800.00. This website was an information only website as my sales agency represents various manufacturing brands. I paid a few hundred dollars here and there for maintenance and updates.

I went two years without having a website. In 2013, I paid over $4,000 for one where I could manage content changes after the initial build out. This was a complete waste of my **MONEY** because I lacked the navigational skills to modify and update content.

In 2019, I operate four informational websites that were super easy to build and are simple to manage and update. My annual cost per year is less than $80.00 per website. I recently purchased my first commerce website (**www.simplebiz360.com**) at an annual cost of $360.00. In all five cases, these **DIY Websites** offer simple building and maintenance templates. I am so happy with their user-friendly formats and yearly costs. What a GREAT way to contain costs and watch my pennies. I strongly suggest you consider researching these cost-effective website building templates. I operate and easily manage content on five websites for less than it cost me for one website in 2008.

MONEY TOOLS 202–233

202. Constantly be aware of **MARGIN EROSION.**
203. Identify, measure and calculate cost **VARIANCES.**
204. Read back all the particulars on **PHONE** orders.
205. **PROCESS** orders promptly.
206. **DISPATCH** invoices promptly.
207. Release invoices on a **TIMELY** basis.
208. Create an invoice **CYCLE** or **RHYTHM.**
209. **VALIDATE** that invoices are properly distributed.
210. Copy yourself on all **EMAIL** invoices.
211. **TRACK** money owed to you by customers.
212. **COLLECT** money owed to you by customers.
213. Create a **BILL OF MATERIALS (BOM)** for each product.
214. Determine **BOM COSTS** for profitable quoting/costing.
215. Track **ACTUAL BOM** costs.
216. Calculate your **HOURLY** value (eight hours per work day).
217. Use **240 BUSINESS DAYS** per year for financial purposes.
218. Manage **BEFORE NINE** time wisely.
219. Plan nine-to-five time with **SPECIFICITY.**
220. Plan healthy life/work balance for **AFTER FIVE** hours.
221. **CONSIDER** working to live rather than living to work.
222. Touch things **ONCE.**
223. Know when/when not to use **MOBILE DEVICES.**
224. Learn how to calculate **GROSS PROFIT MARGIN.**
225. Understand how to calculate **MARKUP.**
226. Establish **INITIAL MARKUP (IMU)** standards.
227. Measure **MAINTAINED MARKUP (MMU)** results.
228. Quantify **FIXED** costs for your business.
229. Identify **VARIABLE** costs for your business.
230. Calculate accurate **COSTS OF GOODS SOLD.**

231. Watch the **PENNIES** over the dollars.

232. Consider **DISCOUNT** travel services.

233. Research and use **DO-IT-YOURSELF** (**DIY**) websites.

Complacency is the
breeding ground for mediocrity.

TOOLS 234–255

SBK = Silent Business Killer

Attitude Increases Altitude

IMPROVEMENT is an attitude that requires an appetite for change. Do you want to grow? Do you want a better return on your investment of time and money? Do you want to earn the same income or strive to make more? Do you want more **Referrals**? If the answer is yes to any or all of these questions, then you are willing to change.

The concept of getting better is the catalyst for this book. **IMPROVEMENT** is the one-word explanation for this book. I learned early in my career that the key to achieving more was to make a commitment to making changes by honing my business skills. If I wanted to raise the altitude of my business achievements, my attitude towards **IMPROVEMENT** was the necessary first step.

In *Managing* by Harold Geneen (1985), this notion of an embedded outlook of striving to improve is described in the following:

> Over the years, this attitude toward work as a creative experience became an ingrained way of thinking for me, and it served me well. I have always tried to find some way of doing things better than I had before, and over the years it has given me an enthusiastic outlook on almost everything.

When I first noticed these words in February 2019, I grinned widely because the words also explain my professional journey. Ever since my 1984 lightbulb moment to embrace training, my career has been a 'creative experience' driven by a thirst to improve. The pilot light on my business stove was lit by Lanier Business Products, and it has never turned off.

My pilot light increased with intensity to a full flame in 1989. While training and managing dozens of nationwide entry-level salespeople, I was thrilled to see when a young salesperson experienced a "got-it" moment. It was so rewarding because I knew that my development leadership helped them to improve. These moments crystalized my understanding of why so many school teachers love what they do. I imagine that many teachers experience great reward when a student understands a concept. This is why in 1989 I decided to write a business book. I wanted to share those "aha!" and "got-it" moments with the business world.

Here are my simplistic suggestions to travel your own original and rewarding path to **IMPROVEMENT**.

The 1% Multiplier

IMPROVEMENT requires a desire to change and escape mediocrity by enhancing your professional skills. This mission does not have to be a cumbersome, daunting task that requires enormous time and energy. Consider this: To improve by 10%, find ten aspects of your business you can improve by 1% each. Improving one component of business by 1% is a simple approach to making you and your business better. Climb the **IMPROVEMENT** ladder one step at a time. You will find that this attitude is rewarding and fun.

Imagine using this 1% approach year after year on different disciplines of your business. The multiplying effect of 1% x 10, or 1% x 15, or 1% x 20 creates and ensures a rewarding business model that delivers you more return on your investment and keeps the **SBKs** far away.

The Power of Three

The logo of this chapter is a triangle. **Why?** The three sides of the triangle represent using the power of three when carving out a game plan to **IMPROVEMENT**. The power of three is another very simple approach to getting better. This three-prong concept consists of "Take-aways," "Minimums" and "Try-its" to be useful. My suggestion is you commit to taking away a minimum of three concepts from each business book you read, business conference you attend, and business podcast you listen to.

Commit to evaluating three **IMPROVEMENT** suggestions for a minimum of 30 days. TRY these three **Tools,** then measure the results of testing these enhancements. Next, APPLY them to your business procedures if you find them beneficial. If you don't like the results of one, two or all three, then don't use them — FRY them!

Continuous Improvement

The concept of **Continuous Improvement** is anchored by a constant quest to be improving. If you approach your career and company as that 'creative experience,' then I invite you to constantly be on the lookout for opportunities to make small enhancements or adjustments for the betterment of your business.

Tom Peters mentions in *The Little BIG Things* (2010) that he spent an entire summer editing his book. This demonstrates supreme dedication and commitment to improving a product. This focus on excellence by Mr. Peters is quite evident in his writing. By the way, this is a great read, and one of many business books he has written. Mr. Peters is a contagious, inspiring and insightful author.

Continuous Improvement can be specific to one discipline of your business, like customer ordering, or it can relate to a daily approach. Let's focus on specificity with orders as our first example. After 60 days, you modified the ordering process four times. Maybe you bought something from a supplier and you admired a certain sentence in their order confirmation. Then, you modified the wording of one of your confirmation sentences. Then, one week later you decided to install the product picture in confirmation notifications. Your use of **Continuous Improvement** is always trying to make the ordering process better.

Now let's focus on **Continuous Improvement** as an overall and general attitude. Today you install the product picture in order confirmations, and tomorrow you will change paragraph two on the website "ABOUT US" tab to better describe your company origins. Later, you decide to buy logo taping for outgoing packages to assist in brand building. Finally, on your drive to a meeting the following day, the lightbulb goes off in your mind and you decide to insert "Thank You" postcards with every outgoing order you send to customers.

My point is this: Periodically examine your business with critical and contemplative reflection. This routine exercise will uncover positive change to **Procedures,** products and services.

Have some fun, and cultivate an enthusiastic outlook similar to Mr. Geneen and many other successful business professionals.

Transferrable Skills

With an attitude oriented toward **IMPROVEMENT,** business owners enhance their operational and managerial abilities when they implement new *SimpleBiz360*™ **Tools.** This can become very helpful if for some reason you close or sell your business. If this business closure or sale happens, you can pack up the **Tools** and take them to your next career capacity. These **IMPROVEMENTS** will be applicable across different companies and industries. These *SimpleBiz360*™ **Tools** will become part of your business DNA no matter what endeavor you pursue.

The development of **Transferrable Skills** was one of my unique selling points while I was recruiting entry-level college graduates to a five-million-dollar company. I consistently encouraged these new-hires to see that this short-term career decision would enable them to acquire various business **Tools** that they would never learn in a Fortune 500–1000 corporation. Encouraging these new-hires, I emphasized how these **Tools** would be transferrable to their future occupations enabling them to earn hearty wages and to become more valuable employees than their Fortune 500–1000 graduate peers.

Best Practices

This term describes business conduct that is considered to be top-shelf in effectiveness. For example, when automated shipment tracking became available, it was a marvel to all of us in business. No more calling, faxing, emailing or hunting and pecking to find out where a shipment was. All of a sudden, we got tracking #'s that we could forward to the customer, and they could find out where their package was at any given moment.

That above scenario became a **Best Practice** for businesses to aspire to. Today, as consumers we feel slighted if we cannot get a tracking number to find out where our shipment is. The shipping industry has raised the bar on deliverables and created a new expectation level that others must live up to. Companies that don't offer this capability are considered behind the times, outdated and the SBK effect is right around the corner waiting to pounce.

As you consider what **IMPROVEMENTS** to make, bend your mind to recall and research companies that behave with **Best Practices**. These companies can be an inspiration for making your changes.

Keep in mind that the majority of the **Tools** taught by *SimpleBiz360*™ are rooted in, and inspired by decades of exposure to **Best Practices.** Our **Tool Chest** is full of operational **IMPROVEMENTS** that went through the exercise of TRY IT, APPLY IT or FRY IT.

Replicate & Duplicate

Expanding on **Best Practices** is **Replicate & Duplicate**, or "**R&D**." Not to be confused with the traditional research & development connotation, **R&D** is a proven path to **IMPROVEMENT**. **R&D** springs up from keen observation of admirable conduct you bump into, interact with, rub shoulders with, read about, hear about or see with your own eyes. You should never plagiarize the procedure or **Tool** word-for-word. However, take the bones and wrap your business components around the structure of a **Best Practice** that gets your attention. This will customize it to your business and assist in the **IMPROVEMENT**.

For example, if you ship product and customers want to track it, then pay attention to bounce back emails you get from other businesses or services. When you see one you really like, to the best of your ability try to emulate it for your business. Perform a little **R&D**, make it fit your business, and TRY IT for 30 days. At day 25, ask some customers what they think about the changes you have made.

At the end of 30 days, either APPLY IT as a standard operating procedure, revise it to incorporate corrective customer feedback, RETRY IT for 30 days or FRY IT.

I was in the fashion private label apparel business in the late 1990's. One of my jobs was to fly to Montreal twice per year to shop for fashion apparel, largely influenced by European designs. Then I was promoted and went to the additional cities of London, Paris and Amsterdam. Our entire mission on each shopping trip was to find fabrics, features, styles, trim, colors and finishes we could use in our merchandising efforts. We were really just performing **R&D** based on what was successful, or perceived to be trendy in other countries. No kidding! Much of the apparel style you buy in the US is replicated and duplicated from European styles a few years old.

There is really nothing new under the sun. This chapter and book contain so many **Tools** that result from testing by generations of professionals that precede *SimpleBiz360*™. I have personally modified many **Tools** for my industry or company compatibility and usage. Once customized, tested and proven, these **IMPROVEMENTS** become worthy partners from which we can all benefit. If we were to dissect the **Tools,** we would find that many of the supporting bones date back long ago. This is the exact reason I chose the tagline **Timeless Business Tools**.

Engage Customers

Current customers are the very best source of information to help you identify potential **IMPROVEMENT** opportunities. Ask them to give you feedback. In return, incentivize them with something for their efforts. Try issuing a 10% discount on their next order, free shipping for one month, or some temporary, extra benefit they receive when they use your business. Keep it simple, and take the burden off their shoulders. You will get solid feedback. Remember, most customers listen to business radio **WIIFM**. They want to know…What's in it for me?

SimpleBiz360™ has incorporated two key questions for customers to assist in the **IMPROVEMENT** identification process. These are found in **Tools 253–254**.

IMPROVEMENT TOOLS 234–255

234. To improve, you must embrace **CHANGE.**

235. View improvement as a **CONTINUOUS** process.

236. **RESEARCH** resources available to help you improve.

237. Establish measurable **TIMELINES** for improvement.

Consider:

238. **CREATING** realistic goals for an improvement initiative.

239. **ACHIEVING** improvement in small, 1% doses.

240. **READING** one pertinent business book per month.

241. **LISTENING** to one pertinent podcast per week.

242. **ATTENDING** one pertinent business seminar per year.

243. **LEARNING** from the past to spark future improvement.

244. **EVALUATE** what social media sites to follow.

245. Identify **SPECIFIC** resources for your improvement goals.

246. **CONSULT** our 255 Tools for improvement opportunities.

247. **IDENTIFY** areas of your company worthy of improvement.

248. **REPLICATE** and adopt best practices from other industries.

249. Periodically **REVIEW** processes for revision opportunities.

250. **RECOGNIZE** what customers want improved.

251. Embrace **ISSUES** as improvement opportunities in disguise.

252. **MEASURE** your hourly worth each quarter.

Incentivize customers to:

253. Communicate what they **DISLIKE** about your business.

254. Share what they would **IMPROVE** about your business.

255. Highlight what they **LIKE** about your business.

Thank You

My sincere hope is that this book will help you do the following:

1) Discover more enjoyment in small business ownership.
2) Retain more of your hard-earned profits.
3) Get a better return on your investment of time and money.

Please accept my sincere gratitude for purchasing this book. I hope you and your family benefit from the content. Remember that we are on the same ground level together. Our common thread is that we share lofty aspirations of business ownership. We are living our dreams. We are wearing many different hats in order to operate our companies. Like many of you, I am bone tired at the end of a week with multiple tasks left on my to-do list on any given day. We juggle and multi-task to make our businesses live on to the next day. I love doing business!

I am blessed to share my journey with you. Introducing solopreneurs and small business owners to the concepts of *SimpleBiz360*™ is an honor and privilege.

Infotainment

Beginning in late 2019, we will explore each **Business Tool** in weekly podcasts. These will feature examples, stories and honest discussion designed to help you improve your company and realize a better return on your investments of time and money. The broadcast format will feature a blend of information and entertainment, **Infotainment**.

Partnership Programs

SOLOPRENEUR PROGRAMS: *SimpleBiz360*™ offers services designed to assist one-person and companies with identification and pursuit of **IMPROVEMENT** opportunities. This is our menu:

1) **Surfing** – 3-month program
2) **Snorkeling** – 6-month program
3) **Scuba Diving** – 12-month program

For **SOLOPRENEUR** program details, please visit the **PROGRAM** tab on **www.simplebiz360.com**.

GROUP PROGRAMS: *SimpleBiz360*™ also offers services designed to assist small companies and small groups in interactive seminar formats. Speaking engagements are also part of our **GROUP** portfolio.

If you are interested in **GROUP** programs, please contact us through our website for details and pricing.

Full Tank & Windows Down

Ever since my 16th birthday, all I needed was a full tank of gas, the windows down, music cranking and miles of open road ahead. Once out of the driveway, my mind would wander and every trip seemed like I was sailing away on some exciting and unique adventure. I still feel that way.

These are the products of my trade. I am stuffed to the gills almost each time I embark on 1000-mile territory journeys in my SUV with 214,000 miles. With me on every trip is my **Tool Chest** complete with eight drawers and **255 Tools**, providing **Guardrails** from the SBKs and paving the way for a quality business ownership experience by satisfying customers.

TOOLS 1–28

Determine what customers:

1. **WANT**.
2. **NEED**.
3. **DESERVE**.
4. DO *NOT* WANT.

5. Create your **INTERNAL EXPECTATION** list.
6. Write a **CUSTOMER EXPECTATION** list.
7. **COMMUNICATE** Customer Expectation List to clients.
8. **CARRY** print copies of your Customer Expectation List.
9. **LAMINATE** and carry your Customer Expectation List.
10. **DISPLAY** customer expectations on your company website.
11. **MEET** or exceed your stated customer expectations.
12. Communicate **COMPLETION/DELIVERY** dates.
13. Provide voluntary **UPDATES** on completion/delivery.
14. Create **REALISTIC** completion/delivery dates.
15. **DEFINE** product and service programs clearly.
16. Provide detail in product **DESCRIPTIONS**.
17. Include **SPECIFICATIONS** in product descriptions.
18. Publish clear **WARRANTY** guidelines.

TOOLS 1–28 (cont'd)

19. Explain **RETURN** policies.
20. Outline processes with step-by-step **DETAIL**.
21. Use **SIMPLE** words in all explanations.
22. **REFLECT** on good and bad customer interactions.
23. Ask customers for their **EXPECTATIONS**.
24. Communicate **IMPROVEMENTS** to your customers.
25. Obtain customer **FEEDBACK**.

Notify customers of your turnaround time for:

26. **RETURN** phone calls.
27. **RETURN** emails.
28. **UPDATES**.

TOOLS 29–47

Operate with:

29: **INTEGRITY.**

30: **HONESTY.**

31: **CONSISTENCY.**

32: **RELIABILITY.**

33: **RESPECT.**

34. **COURTESY.**

35. **POLITENESS.**

36: **KINDNESS.**

37: **PUNCTUALITY.**

38: **THOROUGHNESS.**

39: **ATTENTION-TO-DETAIL.**

40: **APPROPRIATENESS.**

41: **DEPENDABILITY.**

42: **ACCURACY.**

43: **SINCERITY.**

44: **HUMILITY.**

45: **PRODUCT KNOWLEDGE.**

46. **CLEANLINESS.**

47: Good **HYGIENE.**

TOOLS 48–62

Do the following with your **Core Competency (CC)**:

48. **IDENTIFY.**
49. **PROMOTE.**
50. **POLISH** (Improve/Enhance).
51. Provide **PROOF.**
52. Obtain **TESTIMONIALS.**
53. Establish **REWARDS** for customers who buy your CC.
54. **VALUE** CC with your best time and effort.
55. **REDUCE** CC costs (over time).
56. **INCREASE** the profitability of CC through efficiencies.
57. Continually **MEASURE** the costs of your CC.
58. Know how your **COMPETITION** markets your CC.
59. Identify and market CC **UNIQUENESS.**
60. **COMMUNICATE** your CC uniqueness to customers.
61. **EXPAND** your business around CC as the centerpiece.
62. Establish your core **HALLMARK** and live up to it.

TOOLS 63–94

63. Demonstrate respect for the **TIME** of the customer.

64. Demonstrate respect for the **MONEY** of the customer.

65. Give customers your **UNDIVIDED ATTENTION**.

66. Recognize the customer by **NAME**.

67. Take adequate **NOTES** while working with customers.

68. Keep **POLITICS** out of customer interactions.

69. Create **EASY-TO-USE** on-line customer products and services.

70. Find ways to **THANK** customers often.

71. Express customer appreciation with **SINCERITY**.

72. **LEARN** a little about your customer.

73. Demonstrate genuine **INTEREST** in the life of your customer.

74: **RECIPROCATE** when customers show interest in your life.

75. Work on being **LIKEABLE.**

76. **ELIMINATE** conduct that creates customer tension.

77. **DRESS** in industry appropriate apparel.

78. **GROOM** in an industry appropriate manner.

79. Use appropriate **TABLE MANNERS**.

80. Answer the customer question: **What's in it for me (WIIFM)?**

81. Understand the five-step **BUYING PROCESS.**

82. Ask for the business (**DIRECT** or **ALTERNATE**).

83. Don't take a customer **NO** personally.

TOOLS 63–94 (cont'd)

84. Be prepared for **NO ANSWER** (the new no).
85. Understand how **Evidence DEFEATS Disbelief**.
86. Learn to become **COMFORTABLE** using evidence.
87. Create and use a business **TRAVEL** proof/evidence portfolio.
88. Create and use a business **CYBER** proof/evidence portfolio.
89. Develop an **APPRECIATION PROGRAM** for customers.
90. Devote **FRIDAY AFTERNOONS** to checking on customers.
91. Learn to volunteer an **APOLOGY** when necessary.
92. Resolve conflicts **FACTUALLY**, not emotionally.
93. Build issue resolution on **REALISTIC** capabilities.
94. Choose your words and **SPEAKING TONE** carefully.

TOOLS 95–137

Create the following:

95. **ORDER ENTRY** instructions (step-by-step).
96. Product warehouse **PACKING** instructions (step-by-step).
97. Product **RETURN** instructions (step-by-step).
98. **ISSUE RESOLUTION** format.
99. Descriptive **WARRANTY** policy.
100. **QUOTE** template for quick, consistent use.
101. Content **PROTOCOLS** for issuing written quotes.
102. In-house **AUDIT** protocols to ensure consistency.
103. **QUALITY CONTROL** protocols ensure consistent quality.
104. User-friendly and effective **CREDIT APPLICATIONS**.
105. **ONE-TOUCH** management protocols.
106. **ELECTRONIC** file cabinets for each customer.
107. Informative and polite **VOICEMAIL** message.
108. **SELL SHEETS** for all primary products.
109. Flyer **TEMPLATES** for consistency and rapid design.
110. **NEW PRODUCT** flyers for invoices and product shipments.
111. Consistent **INVOICE RELEASE** protocols.
112. **PUNCTUAL** invoice distribution protocols.
113. Customer-friendly product **TERMINOLOGY**.

TOOLS 95–137 (cont'd)

114. **ITEM #s** for all products and services.

115. Marry **EXPECTATIONS** and **PROCEDURES**.

116. Consider **NOTE JOURNALS** for long-term record keeping.

117. Set up **EMAIL TEMPLATES** for future time conservation.

118. Embed **BRAND MESSAGING** wherever appropriate.

119. Include **COUNTRY OF ORIGIN** on all packaging.

120. Commit to **ANSWER** 100% of inbox emails consistently.

121. **SORT** and **FILE** emails on a regular basis.

122. **USE** consistent product terminology.

123. **DISPLAY** item #'s on all print and digital platforms.

Wholesaler Procedure Tools:

124. Create hi-resolution **DIGITAL ASSETS** for all products.

125. Set up a **DIGITAL ASSET MANAGEMENT (DAM)** site.

126. Establish consistent layout **FORMAT** for digital assets.

127. **ASSIGN** edition #s to each print or digital catalog.

128. Invest in **PURCHASING** authentic UPC codes.

129. Obtain authentic **G1 CERTIFICATES** for UPC codes.

130. Apply **DUAL** UPC label for retail + ecommerce.

TOOLS 95–137 (cont'd)

131. Ensure UPC codes are also **HUMAN READABLE (HR)**.

132. Affix HR + Barcode UPCs on **INNER** product packaging.

133. Place HR + Barcode UPCs on **OUTER** product packaging.

134. **PRE-TEST** UPC barcode labeling to ensure reliable scanning.

135. Apply **PROP 65** labeling on all applicable products.

136. Use hi-resolution **IMAGERY** for each color (no color chips).

137. Develop user-friendly **ON-LINE** ordering processes.

TOOLS 138–163

138. **GET** to the customer before they get to you.

139. Tell the customer what they **DESERVE** to hear.

140. Deliver prompt **FOLLOW-UP**.

141. Deliver competent **FOLLOW-THROUGH**.

142. Use **PROFESSIONAL** words and attitude.

143. Learn **HOW** to say things with diligence and care.

144. Tune into the customer radio station **WIIFM**.

145. **VOLUNTEER** customer service information.

146. **ACKNOWLEDGE** receipt of email or phone inquiries.

147. Provide quality **RESPONSES** to email or phone inquiries.

148. **UPDATE** customers on your service efforts and results.

149. **CONFIRM** one-on-one conversations in writing.

150. Maintain a **WRITTEN** job trail, preferably email.

151. Avoid providing **SWIICFU** service.

152. Read customer orders **CAREFULLY** to avoid errors.

153. Leave call-back expectations on **VOICEMAIL** messages.

154. Install your **COMPANY NAME** on voicemail messages.

155. Know **HOW** you service leaves good or bad impressions.

156. Service customers with **TRUTH** and not smokescreens.

TOOLS 138–163 (cont'd)

157. Realize that customers **DETECT** lies easily.

158. Be respectful and polite with Customer **CARE.**

159. **MINIMIZE** customer involvement with service tasks.

160. Learn to **APOLOGIZE** quickly and emphatically.

161. Use **SINCERITY** when apologizing.

162. Pay attention to customer **BODY LANGUAGE**.

163. Learn to say **NO** politely.

TOOLS 164–201

164. Answer **100%** of inquiries you receive.

165. Respond to inquiries in a **TIMELY** manner.

166. Read all electronic **ATTACHMENTS** carefully.

167. Read the **ENTIRE** email that is sent with attachments.

168. Answer questions with **DIRECT** responses.

169. Provide **COURTESY COMMUNICATION (C-COM).**

170. Remove anxiety by using the CPA method when **WRITING.**

171. Remove anxiety by using the CPA method when **TALKING.**

172. Think like the **READER** when writing emails and letters.

173. Express **CONFIDENCE** (not arrogance).

174. Demonstrate **SINCERITY.**

175. Write **CLEARLY.**

176. Use **SIMPLE** words when writing.

177. Explain **WHY** in your correspondence.

178. Use the word **WE** in place of I.

179. Number **REQUESTS & QUESTIONS.**

180. List **DATES** in completion/delivery correspondence.

181. Name **CARRIERS** (USPS/UPS/FED EX) & **TRACKING** #s.

182. Fully **DESCRIBE** revisions and changes.

183. List **ITEM #s** on correspondence and in marketing.

184. Write emails with mission-specific **SUBJECT** titles.

TOOLS 164–201 (cont'd)

185. **SEGMENT** different topics in singular correspondence.

186. Send **MEETING RECAPS** after meetings and discussions.

187. Erase internal email trails before **FORWARDING** externally.

188. Write **COMPREHENSIVE** emails to reduce future questions.

189. **OMIT** opinion in business social media posts.

190. Use social media accounts **WISELY** and **RESPONSIBLY.**

191. **HEAR** what customers are saying.

192. **LISTEN** to what customers are saying.

193. Learn to sincerely **SMILE** face-to-face or on the phone.

194. Make consistent **EYE CONTACT** in face-to-face meetings.

195. Organize electronic information by **TOPIC** or **CUSTOMER.**

196. **SAVE** important sent emails in electronic files.

197. **REPURPOSE** announcement or marketing emails.

198. Practice **REVISING** critical emails before releasing.

199. Save critical emails **OVERNIGHT** for next day perspective.

200. **RELEASE** final, critical emails in mornings for sharpness.

201. Include **CONTACT** information in electronic signatures.

TOOLS 202–233

202. Constantly be aware of **MARGIN EROSION.**

203. Identify, measure and calculate cost **VARIANCES.**

204. Read back all the particulars on **PHONE** orders.

205. **PROCESS** orders promptly.

206. **DISPATCH** invoices promptly.

207. Release invoices on a **TIMELY** basis.

208. Create an invoice **CYCLE** or **RHYTHM.**

209. **VALIDATE** that invoices are properly distributed.

210. Copy yourself on all **EMAIL** invoices.

211. **TRACK** money owed to you by customers.

212. **COLLECT** money owed to you by customers.

213. Create a **BILL OF MATERIALS (BOM)** for each product.

214. Determine **BOM COSTS** for profitable quoting/costing.

215. Track **ACTUAL BOM** costs.

216. Calculate your **HOURLY** value (eight hours per work day).

217. Use **240 BUSINESS DAYS** per year for financial purposes.

218. Manage **BEFORE NINE** time wisely.

219. Plan nine-to-five time with **SPECIFICITY.**

220. Plan healthy life/work balance for **AFTER FIVE** hours.

221. **CONSIDER** working to live rather than living to work.

222. Touch things **ONCE.**

TOOLS 202–233 (cont'd)

223. Know when/when not to use **MOBILE DEVICES**.

224. Learn how to calculate **GROSS PROFIT MARGIN**.

225. Understand how to calculate **MARKUP**.

226. Establish **INITIAL MARKUP (IMU)** standards.

227. Measure **MAINTAINED MARKUP (MMU)** results.

228. Quantify **FIXED** costs for your business.

229. Identify **VARIABLE** costs for your business.

230. Calculate accurate **COSTS OF GOODS SOLD**.

231. Watch the **PENNIES** over the dollars.

232. Consider **DISCOUNT** travel services.

233. Research and use **DO-IT-YOURSELF (DIY)** websites.

TOOLS 234–255

234. To improve, you must embrace **CHANGE.**

235. View improvement as a **CONTINUOUS** process.

236. **RESEARCH** resources available to help you improve.

237. Establish measurable **TIMELINES** for improvement.

Consider:

238. **CREATING** realistic goals for an improvement initiative.

239. **ACHIEVING** improvement in small, 1% doses.

240. **READING** one pertinent business book per month.

241. **LISTENING** to one pertinent podcast per week.

242. **ATTENDING** one pertinent business seminar per year.

243. **LEARNING** from the past to spark future improvement.

244. **EVALUATE** what social media sites to follow.

245. Identify **SPECIFIC** resources for your improvement goals.

246. **CONSULT** our 255 Tools for improvement opportunities.

247. **IDENTIFY** areas of your company worthy of improvement.

248. **REPLICATE** and adopt best practices from other industries.

249. Periodically **REVIEW** processes for revision opportunities.

250. **RECOGNIZE** what customers want improved.

TOOLS 234–255 (cont'd)

251. Embrace **ISSUES** as improvement opportunities in disguise.
252. **MEASURE** your hourly worth each quarter.

Incentivize customers to:

253. Communicate what they **DISLIKE** about your business.
254. Share what they would **IMPROVE** about your business.
255. Highlight what they **LIKE** about your business.

Acknowledgments

I would be nowhere without the love, grace and forgiveness of God. Thank you, God, for leaving us your Word and giving us your Son. Thank you for my sobriety. My family and I stand in awe of your provisions and never-ending Love. Jesus, thank you for saving me and being with me each day. Your love, your actions and your words are the benchmark for my life.

To Monica, you are everything to me. To think that day after day I have the privilege of being your husband. I so deeply appreciate your sticking with me during my rascal days of alcohol addiction. Your counsel, wisdom, clarity, common sense and beauty are sensational. God was smiling down on me when I was introduced to you. I love you and thank you for loving our kids so much. Thanks for putting up with all my travel, dealing with my long work days and supporting me in my dreams to share this book's simple principles with the world.

To Marisa and Amanda, I love you girls and I am honored to be your dad. You complete me and give us so much joy. I am so proud of both of you. Mom and I are very thankful that you live so close and for supporting my dream.

Mom and Dad, thank you for raising me in a good home with values to succeed in life. Your love and support are deeply appreciated. Thank you, Marcia and Cindy, for being such cool sisters who I love very much. Watching your kids grow is exciting, and I am blessed to be their uncle.

To Shorty, I am so appreciative of the time, effort and money you have poured into our family. I love you and am excited that you get to be so close to your daughter, grandchildren and great-grandchildren.

I am proud of you Dan, and most important, thankful in knowing how much you love God, our daughter and your two awesome kids. Mason and Logan, you have brightened the world of Nana and Popi beyond anything words can describe. I love you tons and look forward to every minute we spend together.

A shout-out goes to Russell Eberhart for stopping to talk with us on the beach. Our conversation made all the difference with this manuscript. Best wishes with your writing endeavors. Many, many thanks to LeeAnna Groves for editing this manuscript. What a tremendous pleasure it is to work with you. You are more like my writing coach than an editor. Thank you for believing in this project, for making me a better writer and for your straightforward approach.

Michael Lode, thank you for a great cover and author picture. Your friendship is special, and I appreciate all those years of demonstrating what a "realistic" retail buyer looks like. Bob Zelle, you do terrific work, and I appreciate your help with my brands. You get my vision and your execution is phenomenal. Go Blues!

Sister Carolyn, Sister Michelle, Sister Mary, Sister Ann Margaret and Sister Malia: Thank you for your hospitality and the wonderful cabins at Windridge Solitude (**windridgesolitude.org**). I can't wait to come back.

To Peter Scardino, I have complete admiration for you. Thanks for always having my back and for enduring that legendary meeting at Kohl's. I'll never forget your encouraging comment on my last day, and the fact that you took the elevator back up to our floor just to tell me what you thought. You made my eight years at Oxford a top-shelf, professional experience. I was honored to work with you and for you. Thanks for writing the foreword.

Please accept my sincere appreciation to everyone who took the time to write reviews. Thank you Michael Miller, Mitzi Perdue, Bob Lilly, Jr., Kevin Moran, Nina Brundell, Kyle Reise, Rich Brown, "Jimmy H.," Gregg Koenig, Scott Adams, Gretchen Waterman, Greg Alexander, Adam Mason, Dawn Giombetti, David Giombetti, Didier Villard and Steve Crawford.

So many important people have played impactful roles in my life, creative confidence and evolution in business. Thank you, Gerald Benton, for teaching me that actions have consequences. Thank you to the following staff at Stockton University (previously Stockton State College): Nancy Iszard, James Ewars, Allen B. Edwards Jr. and Dr. Martin L. Needleman. Many thanks go out to Dale Carnegie, Frank Bettger, Tom Peters, Ken Blanchard, Terry McManus, Morris Asch, Steve Arcoleo, Anthony Londino, Walter Sherwood, Chris Garrity, Guy Vincel, Leo J. McDonough, Dale Pisarcik, Seth Lewis, Dr. Susan Rosenthal, Jeff Streader, Jeff Dow, Carolyn Maki, Sigmund Canales, Dennis Rabineau, Ron Cathcart, Kerry Adams, Greg Wiser, Wayne Arnold, Karen Herrick, Mike McGovern, Sheri Gould, Doug Gould, Jim Guntli, Jane Hoepfinger, Kemp Shoun, Sol Jacobs, Jon Van Manen, Bob Carpenter, Chad Weinman, Andrew Hoefener, Erica Schaaf, Jenny Kendall, Beth Frazier-Lynn, John Ruddiman, Hal Moran, Randy Hudson, Doug Gittus, Valerie Brosseau, Lorie DeWorken and the MTM team. Thanks go to John, Joanne, Louis, Isabel and both of your families for being terrific neighbors.

I deeply appreciate all the fine men and women who have served and sacrificed to maintain the freedoms we experience in the United States of America. Thank you for all you have done and continue to do.

My career journeys have allowed me to travel extensively within 49 of our 50 states. I can tell anyone firsthand — we live in a special place full of natural splendor. America is truly beautiful. I love our flag, and I love our wonderful country. God bless America!

**From left to right: Marisa, Shorty, Monica,
Mason, Jeff, Dan, Amanda and Logan. I love you!**

I love the USA!

My favorite writing cabin at Windridge Solitude.

References

Batterson, Mark (2011). *The Circle Maker.* Nashville, TN: HarperCollins Christian Publishing.

Bedbury, Scott with Stephen Fenichell (2002). *A New Brand World.* New York, NY: Viking Penguin Publishing.

Bettger, Frank (1947). *How I Raised Myself from Failure to Success in Selling.* Upper Saddle River, NJ: Prentice-Hall Press.

Blanchard, Ken and Sheldon Bowles (1993). *Raving Fans.* New York, NY: William Morrow and Company, Inc.

Carnegie, Dale (1936). *How To Win Friends & Influence People.* New York, NY: Simon and Schuster, Inc.

Geneen, Harold with Alvin Moscow (1985). *Managing.* New York, NY: Avon Books.

Perdue, Mitzi (2015). *Tough Man, Tender Chicken, Business & Life Lessons from Frank Perdue.* Washington, DC: R. J. Myers Publishing Company.

Peters, Tom (2010). *The Little BIG Things.* New York, NY: HarperCollins Publishing.

Rogers, Buck with Robert Shook (1986). *The IBM Way.* New York, NY: Harper and Row, Publishers, Inc.

Small Business Administration (SBA) Office of Advocacy Report (September 2012). "Frequently Asked Questions About Small Business." Retrieved April 27, 2017, from https://www.sba.gov/sites/default/files/FAQ_Sept_2012.pdf

Technical Assistance Research Program (1985). "Consumer Complaint Handling in America: An Update Study." Washington, DC: Technical Assistance Research Programs Institute.

Walton, Sam with John Huey (1992). *SAM WALTON Made in America.* New York, NY: Doubleday.

Whiteley, Richard C., The Forum Corporation (1991). *The Customer Driven Company.* Reading, MA: Addison-Wesley.

Made in the
USA
Lexington, KY